Praise for A Brave Nev

C000000299

This insightful book is a must read for every CEC
Angela Brav, CEO, In

Colin has that rare ability to summarize and present the essential structure and must-haves of modern business. His new book is another excellent example of his unique laser-sharp thinking.

Doctor George Nagy, CEO, EuroGate

For busy CEOs who seldom have time to read and digest weighty business tomes, Colin's latest book will come as a breath of fresh air. He is a master at crystallizing nuggets of business wisdom into a few short sentences. His words enlighten, inspire and motivate. Enjoy a chapter a day and keep the business blues away!

Gordon Beattie, Chairman, Beattie Communications Group

What distinguishes leaders/winners long-term is the way they think and their attitudes. Winners don't get more opportunities, they create them. This book shares the simple wisdoms that get you there.

Paul Polman, CEO, Unilever

As insightful as ever, simplifying the business world so we can understand what we should be doing, removing the interference in our thoughts. Great book.

Stephen Hucklesby, CEO, Paragon Automotive Group

Insightful and intelligent. A bite sized resource with plenty of fizz.

James Berresford, CEO, Visit England

My interest in Colin was sparked by his weekly CEO Bullet; each missive was delightfully concise, simple and relevant, yet penetratingly thoughtful, stimulating and challenging. The hallmark of anyone at the top of their game is the ability to distil and communicate complexity into simplicity. The impact of Colin's input has been material and that we have been able to sustain the shift to a higher level of strategic and operational ability is a credit to Colin, his insight and the sheer energy he brings to a CEO and teams.

Rick de Blaby, CEO, MEPC

Matt

A BRAVE
NEW BUSINESS
WORLD

With Best Wishes

88 NOTES FOR CEOs

COLIN
TURNER

This Edition Published in UK 2013 by
21st Century Books, London

Typeset by Taylor Thorne Print Ltd, UK

Printed and Bound in Great Britain
By CPI Group, UK

ISBN 978-1-904956-77-8
e-book ISBN 978-1-904956-78-5

CONTENTS

Before Note

After…

Striving to start in the 1973-75 double-dip recession with stagflation…
thriving during the 1980-82 recession at 17% base rates and 60% tax…
surviving the 1990-92 recession when values crashed 70%...
guiding businesses during the 2001 challenges when the world changed…
predicting the 2008 credit crunch when the world fell apart and…
devising strategic Game-Changers for future growth…these
advising notes for CEOs are…
providing ideas and insights to courageously embrace…
A Brave New Business World

Being a CEO is about Guardianship, Stewardship and Responsibility. It involves having the courage to do whatever is demanded, taking the initiative whenever it is required, applying the judgement and experience to back it up, consistently following it through and reliably getting it done.

Recessions are not a natural phenomenon, they are Man-Made: the result of misguided strategy, misinformed decisions and misplaced judgement. History records, however, that the worst of times are the ideal stimulus for the best of times. Challenges stimulate us to search for better ways. To have answers to support a required change in our thinking.

Consider, for example, three questions:

Why does your company really want you?

What business is your company really in?

What legacy will your company really remember you for?

New thinking demands acting with local diligence even when global in scope. The same principles apply from the corner shop to the multi-national corporation: the fundamental purpose of a business being to attract and retain customers while making a profit. Those that declare they are different to other businesses are missing the point of what business is really about.

Yet the world has changed. Customers no longer tolerate being treated as a transaction. There are new realities and new opportunities and the very essence of business has focused into a customer centric purpose: To attract customers and create consumers that repeatedly return, refer and recommend you, because you serve them better than any one else, and make a profit in the process.

Focusing on what must be undertaken to achieve this demands ignoring distractions. None of us have any real influence over distracting economic disturbances. Yet each of us has direct influence over what we do in our day-to-day business. We can choose either to take responsibility or to apportion blame. Put simply if we carry on doing what we have continued to do, we will carry on getting the same result.

Sustainable growth is not built on hindsight, followed by blame and enquiry. We must build with foresight. CEO, Steve Jobs was intent on making 'a dent in the universe,' not for power and glory, but to make a difference. His legacy changed the world. He ignored the '1,000 daily distractions' and despite waves of criticism his products swept over the world: stores recording historic retail highs, while his company became the largest in capital terms ever to date. Following the crowd is not an option for CEOs intent on making a difference.

Over 5,000 CEOs read my weekly missives and many directly communicate confirming that they resonate with them. Some become valued clients – and I welcome this opportunity to thank them all for choosing me to help them make a difference. I further appreciate their requests and encouragement to encapsulate a compilation of selected Colin Turner CEO Bullets with additional insights and ideas that support CEOs embracing a brave new business world that is evolving out of an unviable one.

Successful CEOs have 3 things in common: Resolve, Discipline and Frustration. The first 2 are vital in leadership; Frustration however, is that latent force, when transformed into Fascination for what can and will be achieved, makes the difference. Transformation comes from inspiring ideas and insights that stimulate Strategic Game-Changers that grow the company to the benefit of all Stakeholders. Implementing these Strategic Game-Changers is the No. 1 responsibility of a CEO.

That is why your company really wants you – to bring and deliver value: Value: measured in consistent percentage terms in brand reputation and profitable growth.

It is my intent that these notes will inspire and guide you as a CEO to channel that legacy-making force that transforms your company into everything it has the potential to achieve.

Let's go invent tomorrow
rather than worrying about
what happened yesterday

Steve Jobs

1 Wise & Prudent

The wise CEO harnesses the worst of times…
to be the stimulus towards the best of times:
1. Realising that challenges demand changes…
in planning and following through.
2. Knowing that products or services that do not deliver value…
will no longer be tolerated.
3. Understanding that sustained success is only won…
through consistent reliability.
4. Accepting that the purpose of a business…
is to attract and retain customers.

Challenging times offer greater opportunity…
for the prudent CEO to attract and retain customers…
And how is it they do it?
By making and delivering on marketing promises…
By winning customer approval for the value delivered…
supported by transparent guarantees.
By transforming customers into loyal ambassadors…
willing to refer friends and family…
And then, importantly…
by simply asking them to do so.

Stop thinking in terms of increasing Customers Sales…
Start thinking in terms of increasing Customers Buys.

2 Breaking Boundaries

Mistakes mark progress towards our success…
Indeed every walk to success involves falling over:
Success is a result of good judgment…
Good judgement comes from experience…
Experience is earned through poor judgment…
Poor judgement leads to failure…
Failure is vital to success.
Life is about taking risks and making mistakes…
whether crossing the street or commencing a venture.
Business can offer a world of excitement, status and wealth;
or a closed arena with fixed boundaries…
with the fear of loss and ruin beyond.

Real freedom belongs to those that make a decision.
What is that decision?
It is to break through existing boundaries…
To know what is expected of you and know that you can achieve it…
Knowing that to get something you never had…
you have to do something you never did.

The future must never be considered an extension of the past. Failing at something once, does not mean failure in the future. Not having tried something before does not presuppose that you will not be able to do it.

At any moment you are much more than the sum total of everything you have ever done. Many of the things that you have already achieved were completed despite the uncertainty that you may not, might not, or could not achieve them before you started.

Mistakes mark progress; failing at something is a vital ingredient to succeeding at it. Good judgment comes from experience and experience in turn is based on bad judgment, which leads to mistakes and failure.

Whenever you have the desire to do something different, to jump boundaries, the inevitable chasm appears. Your rationale that occupies a fixed boundary founded on well-meaning admonitions such as 'take-care' warnings, will strive to influence you so that you 'should not bite off more than you can chew.' Your intuition, which knows no boundaries, counsels that you must take the jump – but with a proviso of either: Yes, you can do this; it is the challenge you must take and you are ready, so go-ahead; or, Yes, this is the right challenge, yet the timing is not yet right – get prepared and plan the jump; don't just leap impulsively.

Whenever the thought and desire are in harmony with your abilities and potential your intuition will answer in the affirmative. Whenever the moves you consider making are not in line with your motives, then your intuition will always counsel cautiously. Whenever you are doing something that takes you away from what you have desired to achieve, then you have allowed your own worst enemy to take control of your thinking. The CEO that is unprepared or impulsively leaps to conclusions is acting against the company's best interests.

Life is about taking risks, whether crossing the street or borrowing for a new venture. The key is being fully prepared and aware of the risk to be undertaken. Accidents don't just happen. Human unpreparedness, negligence, lack of awareness and error are the cause. Business is the great arena that offers thrills, excitement, fame, riches, status and success; as well as disaster, ruin, loss, fear and failure. Many remain in the fixed boundaries of the arena. For freedom beyond the walled boundaries only belongs to those prepared gladiators determined to break though, knowing that the key to do so lies deep within themselves, and available to them whenever they make a decision.

What is that decision? It is to break through existing boundaries, indeed to accept no boundaries. To leap when you must without hesitation, because you have already peered over the edge, and you know what is expected of you and you know that you can achieve it.

When you prepare yourself and are prepared to do whatever it takes, then you discover that every challenging chasm that you encounter shrinks as you unhesitatingly leap across it. And remember, to get something you never had you have to do something you never did, so bite off more than you can chew...then chew it.

3 Going Far

All great accomplishments are the result of a continuum of...
a vision held in clear focus by...
a commitment to follow through on...
a shared strategy supported by...
a plan of operational goals measured with...
a series of metrics that inexorably lead to...
a realisation of expectations that exceed...
a reality of a fulfilled vision.

What is really involved?
Flexible Resilience with Agile Thinking and Resolute Focus:
Flexible Resilience is not about Short-termism.
Agile Thinking is not about Opportunism.
Resolute Focus is not about Authoritarianism.
Short-term, opportunistic, high-handedness leads to...
Excessiveness...
Shallowness...
and Bailouts.
Long-term, value-based, determination leads to...
Excellence...
Soundness...
and Accomplishment.
When you pursue a winning business strategy and apply...
Flexible-resilience with Agile-thinking and Resolute-focus...
Your company goes F.A.R.

4
Real Resolve

Successful people know that the price of success…
has to be paid in full and…
has to be paid in advance…
there is no free lunch.
There are sacrifices to make…
There is a cost that must be willingly made.
A cost that proves to be comparatively small…
when measured against the longer-term success realised.
A key determinant of success is calculating the price in advance…
This prepares you physiologically and psychologically…
in terms of resolve…
and discipline, in the same way you prepare yourself…
to pick up a bar bell.
Focusing on the expected benefits puts the price into proportion…
It supports making the decision acceptable…
And sustaining a firm resolve.

THINK BIG…
Because the price for achieving poor results…
is higher than the cost for achieving extraordinary results.
Look upon setbacks as costs to be paid before you get what you want.
View every obstacle as opportunities to build your resolve.
The resolve to keep going until you win through!

A young man dreamed of being a farmer and in due course he found a farm and bought it. Inexperienced in business, he discovered to his horror, after completing his purchase, that there would be insufficient water to irrigate his produce. The river appeared to have dried up overnight.

Following the dried-up riverbed towards its source led him up a mountainous path. In time he came across an enormous boulder that had fallen directly into the path of the river, causing the water to divert its flow to the rocks below where it was lost. He resolved to smash this obstacle to his dreams and returned to his farm to get a sledgehammer. He would have to remove the obstacle on his own for there was no spare money to do otherwise. Upon his return he hit the rock hard, swinging with all his strength. Nothing happened. Not even a mark. Not even a tiny splinter of rock. It was as if he had not even hit it. He hit it again and again and again.

For over 500 times he kept hitting it. His hands had long since blistered and were now bleeding. His chest and shoulders ached from the work. A cry of frustration escaped his lips as he sank to his knees with exhaustion. The boulder stood as it had since the first hit. The farmer started to question his resolve. He started to doubt whether he could ever move it. He began to question whether he should have bought the farm. He began to doubt if he should have even been a farmer. Perhaps his family and friends had been right: His dream was doomed to failure before he started.

If you question anything too long then you start to doubt. After a break he stood up to hit it again, and again. Upon the 502nd time the rock seem to groan before splitting right in two. Instantly the trapped water gushed through. What did it? The 502nd hit, or the 502 hits. We don't always get what we want straightaway. We have to keep chipping away and chipping away until we win through. Too many stop when they have almost succeeded.

What really did it was the farmer's resolve. With such commitment, providence moved. Obstacles instruct more than they obstruct. To be a success you have to believe in yourself, and you have to do what you must do when you should do it, and keep on doing it till you win through.

You have to commit yourself to keep going not when it is easy but when it is tough. When the going is really tough. When everything inside you is telling you to give up. Providence moves on the side of steadfast commitment. Whatever your goal, make a decision that you will never give up on it. Look upon setbacks as lessons that you must endure before you can become what you want. Don't let self-created obstacles of self-doubt defeat you before you start. Resolve to keep going until you win through!

5 Sustaining Resolutions

Making and keeping personal changes at New Year…
has similar challenges to company planning:
Too many resolutions and not enough goals.
A resolution is not a goal.
Resolutions, like strategic missions, work better when…
there are only one or two to focus on.

Success in personal goals and business objectives is achieved…
when they are aligned to resolutions or strategic missions respectively.
A resolution, for example, is a Life-Changer…
with goals being measuring tools to support it.
A strategic mission can be a Game-Changer…
with objectives being supporting tools.
Too many resolutions and commitment quickly wanes…
Too few unspecific goals and persistence weakens.

What to do?
Choose what is really important and…
makes the most measurable difference.
Then align challenging yet measurable goals to ensure…
that what you have resolved to do is sustained.

6 Positioning Propositions

An alarming reality is that when challenged…
most businesses have little idea what makes them stand out.
Determining, defining, articulating and communicating…
Propositions that set you apart…
is the secret to differentiating your business from the competition…
and the very nucleus you build future reputation, …
success and brand upon.

Imagine your customer asking you 4 questions:
1. Selling Proposition:
Why would I, your customer, choose your brand before any other?
2. Value Proposition:
How will I gain value with you versus your cheaper competitor?
3. Reassurance Proposition:
What guarantee do you offer that sets you apart from the rest?
4. Experience Proposition:
What lifestyle element do you offer that attracts me?

These Propositions are not slogans…
They are NOT about you, your business or your profession...
They are about the people that build your reputation, success…
and brand…
YOUR Customer.

Ask most executives what sets their company apart and they momentarily freeze before saying something indistinct and unappealing that does not share the key elements that differentiates them.

The most effective way to get your business noticed and differentiated is by defining and applying your Unique Selling or Service Propositions (USP). When developed they challenge the business to go that extra mile, to make what was impossible possible, and to revolutionize their industry by identifying a uniqueness and harnessing it throughout every marketing campaign. For example the value proposition of FedEx was: 'When your package absolutely, positively has to get there overnight'

This became the very nucleus they built their business success and professional reputation around: It articulated precisely and communicated concisely what they were about. In creating your own:

1. Think in terms of the end-result your customers desire from you.
2. Think in terms of the customer's need you fulfil.
3. Think in Terms of what differentiates you from everyone else.
4. Think in terms of endorsement/what existing customers testify.
5. Think in terms of a compelling headline.
6. Think in terms of what makes you special in your customer's eyes?

Your USP will not appeal to everyone – you are seeking to appeal to those customers from your target market niche. A niche you must identify and profile. You know for certain that your USP is the right one for capturing the hearts and minds of your customers when revenue improves.

Contact customers, remind them of your USP and ask if it influenced their purchasing decisions. Remind customers of the benefits you provide and why you adopted your USP. In doing so you are giving your customer the opportunity to appreciate why you are doing what you are for them. This makes the customer feel valued, confirms their decision to buy from you, makes them feel good about their purchase and prompts them to readily agree to recommend you when you follow up in due course asking for referrals. In doing this you enhance customers' perception of your USP.

Your USP is not about you, your business or your profession. It is all about your customer or your client. They are the ones that build your reputation and success. For example:

"Fresh, hot pizza delivered to your door in 30 minutes or less - or it's free."

Domino's Pizza does not make the best, most delicious, healthy or cheapest pizza...yet it transformed from a small operator into a Billion Dollar Business with a Value Proposition that perfectly encapsulated: Benefit, What it is, Service, Promise and Guarantee. In breaking it down:

Benefit: FRESH & HOT
You do not want old or cold – you want it right and ready to eat.

What it is: PIZZA
Says exactly what you are getting.

Service: DELIVERED TO YOUR DOOR
The convenience – so you do not have to even leave home.

Promise: IN 30 MINUTES OR LESS
Gives you a clear expectation.

Guarantee: OR IT'S FREE
Reinforces the promise.

Dominos hold the number 1 position in the pizza market. Yet, the USP makes no claim to be the best pizza, the number one pizza, the best value, the most delicious, or the healthiest. It simply fulfils the plain need of: We're hungry and we can't be bothered to cook.

Apply the same basic elements to your own:
Benefits
What it is
Service
Promise
Guarantee

Don't expect the perfect proposition quickly – they take time, yet when you get it right – you will know it and your business will show it.

7 CEO CMO

Most business plans present a perfect projected profit analysis...
an impressive recipe with every winning ingredient except one...
No customer.
Friends and Family may love your idea...
but will they actually buy it?
Most business plans miss the point.
The real secret of business success...
is not more finance...
it is more custom:
the key determinant for healthy cash flow.

A business can survive without profit...
but not without cash...
The projection of profits is no consolation...
when negative cash flow impacts a business.
A business without custom is not a business.
So plan to attract more customers to generate cash flow.
And when business thrives from renewed good margins...
reinvest profit to attract more custom.
Don't follow the Banking Model of: 'Loans keep business going...'
Rather focus on 'Custom keeps business growing.'

And this is the real point:
CEOs are also CMOs – Chief Marketing Officers...
Because PR & Marketing create customers.

8 Gold Asset

Customers are the life-blood of a company…
they are the cash flow.
Businesses that fully harness their solid gold asset of a Database…
that precisely profile and timely target customers succeed.
Most operate haphazardly, ignoring the valuable Database and bleed…
haemorrhaging from wrong customers that don't buy.
The 2 questions essential to any marketing campaign are…
1. Who is your target market? Identify precisely your audience.
2. What will your business provide it? Identify the specific need you fulfil.

A precision-driven marketing approach…
applying a high-quality list of customers proves profitable.
The untargeted blanket approach that generates low-margins does not.
Quality of leads, based on careful profiling of your customers…
improves your ability to convert them into sales.

Regularly Review your Database…
Reassess Customer Management Relationships.
Reorganise in to Gold, Silver and Bronze Listings.
Remind your people to always go for Gold.

Marketing is not a support tool for selling. It is about building good customer relationships. Good relationships that in time form one of your most valuable golden assets: a Database. Building a Database of customers of one-time buyers, which choose to become life-long customers, because what you deliver is greater than you promise, carries positive benefits and makes them feel valued, is very important.

Many businesses that have been in business for years have NOT kept a database of their valued clients or customers. They continue to earn what they have always done, but they never MAKE money – and LOSE out on potential income because they are continually losing their customers.

Others have a Database, but do not use it. With a Database of just 1000 loyal customers imagine how the launch of a new product or service will be received. A specialist optician, for example, wrote to each of his customers thanking them for their custom over the years and inviting them to try out his latest product range with a pre-launch discount in recognition of their loyalty. The response was so phenomenal that he was left with no new stock for the launch – making more money in one evening than he did in 3 weeks trading.

Whatever business you are in; whatever you do; whatever your role; your revenue and profits are either directly or indirectly generated because of somebody exchanging money for a form of service or product that you are directly or indirectly involved with.

If you do not have a Database, then start building one.
If you do have a Database, then review, clean, build and use it regularly.

9 Curve Learning

70 businesses fail every day in the UK. (Experian Credit Report).

Statistics heartily reported by Media to confirm how 'bad things are'...
Yet when placed into an alternative percentage context...
This represented less than 0.1% of businesses...
To put another way: 99.9% strived to succeed.

Where business is the great arena to test the mettle of courage...
Alarming news is the dismal desert to nettle and discourage.
What counts is that you are the strategic-driven...
master of your business...
not the misguidedly-influenced slave distracted by louder opinions.

For this reason business must be continually monitored...
with simple systems put in place.
Systems that flag up in advance...
when something is leading you in the wrong direction.

Business is about learning from mistakes...
These are the furnaces that temper our mettle into cutting-edge steel.
Without learning curves we remain dull iron.
The secret is to embrace and learn from them, and above all...
harness them towards even greater heights.

10 Follow Basics

Words without reliable follow-through…
ultimately reveal a lack of dedication.
Doing what you believe in…
and making it happen is not easy.
Fulfilling a Company Vision…
Strategic Mission or Operational Objective…
demands much, much, more than talk, talk and more talk.

Procrastination is not starting what is required.
Complacency is doing less than required…
Commitment is doing much more than required…
Dedication is doing whatever it takes.

This is what Authentic Leaders discover deep inside…
when aligning action with what they passionately believe.
That is what following-through is really about:
making things happen…
delivering on promise…
and transforming words into deeds.
Leadership inspires the involvement that ignites commitment…
Authenticity builds commitment into dedication…
Dedication positively influences everything that is good in business…
Ultimately measured by the Top and Bottom line.

When companies become blinkered, motivated by more and more, rather than by basic principles, the bottom line suffers. When the Bottom Line suffers it is because of the Top Line forgetting to apply basics. CEOs must regularly remind themselves of the basics. For business is simple, as success grows we complicate it. Business today too often illustrates Management's ability to complicate simplicity.

The basic principles learned from being raised on a Highland Croft were: Choose your field, prepare the ground, plant at the right time, nurture your produce, reap when ripe, reward and thank any help you received as well as your customers for being regular, reinvest profit in more seed, maybe for some additional land and also for hard times that may suddenly arise in the future, and finally inspect your field. Simple, but if not followed there is no money or food. Without food you go hungry. Similarly if a business is not fuelled, then, quite simply, it fails.

In farming, if there is a problem, you go to the root of the cause. If the seed does not grow, it is not the fault of the seed. It is the fault of badly prepared ground giving a lack of nutrients. If a young plant does not grow, it is not the fault of the plant; it is because of lack of sustenance and general nurturing. The strategy of pulling the plant out of the soil to check on progress will destroy it.

Though the word organisation comes from the word organise, to put things in order; and the place where products are created is called a plant, it is clear that with some organisations the comparison stops. Imagine shareholders metaphorically pulling your plants out of the ground and warning them that if they do not grow faster they will not give them any more water. It is essential that leadership and management do not get bogged down in the minutiae of business.

They must regularly revisit the basics by asking sequential questions as illustrated under the heading of 'Business' in the table below:

Farming	Business	Jargon	
1. Choose field.	Why will this company exist?	Mission	L
2. Prepare the ground.	What are we about?	Values	E
3. Plant at the right time.	Where do we want to go?	Objectives	A
4. Nurture your produce.	What do we have?	Strengths	D
5. Ensure regular irrigation.	How will we get there?	Strategy	E
6. Reap when ripe.	Do we <u>Build Relationships</u>?	Marketing	R
7. Bring to Consumer.	How well are they received	Revenue	S
8. Reward & Thank.	Do we <u>Follow Through</u>?	Service	H
9. Re-invest Profit.	How are we going to expand?	Results	I
10. Re-inspect field.	Is our process working?	Manage	P

In revisiting such basics, leadership can re-sow the seeds of greatness that will recreate them as an entrepreneurial corporation. Relationships fall apart because they forget what brought them together; and too many businesses fail because they ignore basics.

Note that business is about Building Relationships and Following Through: Marketing is not a support tool for selling; it is for building relationships. Service involves following through what you said you would do – about fulfilling what had been promised. Note the position of "Manage." People don't want managing; they want leading. You manage process and things, not people. When the basics are adhered to in the right sequence then authentic leadership happens.

11 Not Price

Spending has changed over 3 generations:
1970s: Spend when you have the money…
1990s: Spend now and pay later…
2010s: Spend? I want it for nothing!

Selling on price has never been a prudent strategy…
for those good companies preferring consistent growth.
In persuading customers today to spend on price alone…
what value statement are you putting out?
Property location proves a better investment than price…
similarly, Positioning in business…
proves a better strategy than Prospecting.
Yet most companies focus on price strategy…
instead of strategic positioning that leads…
to becoming the preferred choice in your field.

What to do?
Take time to develop your Positioning Propositions…
The very essence that positively influences your customer's choice…
to only buy from you, rather than another.
Ultimately the Propositional Values that position you…
are not about you…
your business…
or your industry…
They are about the people that build your reputation and success…
Your Customers.

12 Less More

Many businesses reflect management's ability...
to complicate simplicity...
Complicating a business is easy.
Simplifying a business is hard...
Activity is about complexity and productivity is about simplicity.
Yes, the devil may be in the detail...
but getting bogged down in minutiae is indicative of building busyness...
rather than business building.
Reviewing that core activity of your business...
most responsible for your greatest productivity is a valuable exercise.

And what is the best way to do this?
The simple answer everyone agrees with yet few undertake...
is re-applying the 80/20 Rule:
Because, whichever way you cut it,
80% of your productivity will come from 20% of your effort...
Re-discovering that core element in your business...
and then simplifying it, is key.

The question to ask is:
What is the 20% that is leading to the 80%?
And to understand:
that it is not the hours you put it that count...
but what you put in the hours.

There is an eastern adage: The less you do, the more you achieve. In western terms we refer to this as effective application of The Pareto Principle where:
80% of sales are generated by 20% of sales people.
80% of profits are generated by 20% of products or service.
20% of customers generate 80% of profits.

Economist Vilfredo Pareto's Rule asserts that when 2 sets of data relating to causes and results are analysed there will be a pattern of imbalance. Though a wealth of data is available that proves why The 80/20 Rule will significantly raise your game, in simple terms everything you do in your business (and your life) can be put into 2 categories:

The majority of what you do daily will have little impact on your success. A small minority of what you do will have a significant impact:
Authors accept that the majority of effort provides a minority of income. Consultants know that, on average, 20% of clients generate 80% of profits. Entrepreneurs realise that a few deals deliver more than the majority.

The question to ask is:
What is the minority that is leading to the majority in your business? The answer to this question can never be assumed or guessed. Seriously consider what vital inputs are having the most significant impact on your business, and what trivial many are impeding doing more of the vital few.

When 80/20 thinking is working for you your resulting actions reduce hassle while achieving more reward from less effort.

The 80/20 Principle implies that we:
1. Channel our efforts effectively.
2. Be selective rather than chase every opportunity.
3. Do the things that bring the best return on our expertise.
4. Consider where 20% of our effort can lead to 80% of returns.
5. Introduce the 80/20 Rule to maximize performance, profits and people.
6. Work hardest on elements that work hardest for you.

Do not misinterpret the 80/20 Rule by getting caught up in the numbers. It could be called the 70/10 Rule, if 70% of the results were created by 10% of the inputs. Do not rationalize why it does not apply to your business. One common argument is that by eliminating the wasteful 80%, eventually you'll end up with nothing. This interpretation of the rule misses the point.

Identify an area where despite huge effort there is an imbalance of return. Identify the key 10, 20 or 30 % of inputs that are creating most results. Identify ways to invest time in those activities that produce the best results. Identify how you can eliminate activities that don't deliver a high margin.

13 Good Right

The very essence of what every person ever really wants…
can be reduced down to just 2 vital ingredients…
for the right recipe of home and working life…
What are they?
1. Good Feelings…
and…
2. Right Solutions.

The simplest of answers are the best truths…
and the simple truth is that…
when you provide both of these things at the same time…
your business will consistently become stronger.

The 2 vital keys business must consistently achieve are:
1. Attract and retain customers.
2. Make a healthy profit.
Without customers and profit…
there can be neither re-investment in the business…
nor reward from the business.
Take time to regularly review and reconfirm if your business…
really does provide good feelings and right solutions.
And when it does…
tell the world about how it does.

14 Negotiating

There is a fact of life…

You don't get what you deserve in life…
You get what you negotiate.

When you can walk away from a deal…
Then you own the negotiation.
When you have need…
Then they own you.

There is one rule:
Have a clear purpose of what you want to achieve…
And what you are prepared to concede…
to get what you want.

Most people are not good at negotiating…
including those people sitting across the table from you…
though never under-estimate anyone.
Tenacity overcomes eloquence.

Most negotiations are not necessary…
and are often the excuse for another meeting.
Therefore only deal with decision-makers…
When it involves you or your business.

Negotiation is an interactive process of communication and therefore a learnable skill. An effective negotiator has applied, practiced and honed this skill. Gather information on the other party's position, issues and expectations. Establish objectives and expectations so you are clear about what you will or will not accept.

Establish:

What we want?

What can we justify?

What adjustments will be required?

What tactics will we employ?

What concessions will we make?

What is the best resolution?

Cooperative negotiators are more effective than competitive negotiators.

Maintain Confidence throughout.

People buy confidence: Confidence from knowing the value you bring.

Ask questions and listen carefully and patiently to what is being sought.

Maintain eye contact – it helps to listen and encourages further information.

Demonstrate you understand what is said.

Paraphrase the points made.

Stay attentive for compromise and solutions that are always overlooked.

Listen by note-making and capture new points that arise.

Maintain command –within price range, delivery time or margin.

When it comes to price write it down and pass it across.

It displays thoughtful consideration and allows observation of reaction.

Aim high from the start: easier to play down yet nigh impossible to go up.

Remain flexible in case direction unexpectedly alters…

or alternative objectives arise.

Make concessions to stimulate the other party to respond similarly.

Make concessions conditional on receiving them in return.

Concede reluctantly in small amounts.

Compromise unless it undermines 'walk away' limit you have set.

When saying No, explain the reason why and offer an alternative.

Consider the possibilities generated.

Focus on interests, not positions.

Separate the people from the problem.
Never close an agreement until you are happy.
Know your 'walk away' from the table position.
Pay attention to details, but don't fuss with minutiae.
Timing is important. Neither push hard, nor delay too long.
Take time out to diffuse tension if required.
In closing seek to record the agreement.
Confirm final agreement.
Shake hands and go – prevarication in conversation ignites reconsideration

Maximize your Leverage
Credibility – in position, expertise, connections, personality.
Situational – as to where you sit and hold the meeting.
Resource – where what you offer is what the other party needs or values.

Always be prepared to walk away.
Never allow the deal to own you.

15
Reward Formula

Success involves good ideas and right implementation.
Experienced CEOs know that:
1. A bad idea correctly executed is more successful…
than a brilliant idea never implemented or followed through.
2. Resourceful marketing coupled with right timing reaps…
greater reward than big budgets coupled with bad decisions.
3. Great service is only recommended…
while poor service is always remembered.

To put it formulaically:
$(I + T + M) \times (E + S) = R$
Where, (Idea + Timing + Marketing) x (Execution + Service) = Reward.

However…
there is a vital multiple factor to the formula…
that most businesses forget…
$D + FT \times (I + T + M) \times (E + S) = R$
where D is Decisiveness…
and FT is Following Through.

Without decisive follow-through…
Reward will always be diluted…
or lost.

16 Right Decisions

In business and life there are alternative perceptions…
behind outcomes of either getting by or getting on:
Excuses or Experiences;
Reasons or Results;
Stories or Success
Good decisions form the very core of right outcomes…
Right decisions are made up of two parts…
Yet the part usually relied upon…
is reasoning out why we should not do something.

Rationale is forming an opinion through reasoned explanation…
Intuition is immediate comprehension without reasoning.
The key is to use them as a team…
not one against the other.
Both are necessary to each other as yin to yang:
Good decision-making involves intellect, perception, emotion and intuition.
Put simply:
…does it add up right?
…does it appear right?
…does it feel right?
…does it sound right?
When applied to making right decisions…
these elements must be applied together.

The real art of using intuition is guiding us towards making good judgment, not replace it. Intuition is a capacity that each of us is born with, like the capacity for breathing and eating. When we breathe properly the lymphatic functions essential to our health measurably improve. When we eat properly our mental and emotional wellbeing improves significantly. When we recognize our intuitive guidance our decisions are always right.

The skill is to combine our intuitive capacity together with all the knowledge we have on a matter and make our decision accordingly. There are questions to apply whenever faced with a decision or a situation that requires a decision. The questions are based on the four psychological processes that we engage when we evaluate situations.

The first is: How does this add up?
This involves what you know based on your knowledge and what you are able to research.

The second question is: What do I think about this?
This is influenced by your perception and interpretation.

The third is: How does this decision feel to me?
You will either feel comfortable about it or not.

The final question is: How does this sound?
This accesses how we intuit about the decision to be made.

1. What do I know about this?   (How do the facts add up?)
2. What do I think about this?   (What is my interpretation?)
3. What do I feel about this?   (Are my emotions are affected?)
4. What do I intuit about this?   (Does it sound right?)

The answers add up to making good judgment and right decisions.

17 Buy Value

When sales are needed to cover costs or meet budgets…
the focus is shifted towards price before value.
and when you focus on price,
you choose to get by, rather than get on.
Selling on price means cutting margins…
and low margins lead to losses.
Yet, with competitors lowering prices and consumers seeking best deals…
what can be done?

First, remember…
that customers like to buy, but don't like to be sold to…
that meaningful purchases are bought on value, not price…
that marketing is about building relationships and following through…
that profit is applause for delivering a great performance.

Second…
adopt strategies that raise perceived value…
and deliver thoughtful follow-through service.

Third…
target new customers that fit the profile of those existing customers…
that value the way you value them…

And fourth…
re-invest the profit from the higher margins in delivering…
even better marketing, value and service.

Striving by price leads to dying by price.
Living by value leads to thriving on value.

18 Self Respect

Our greatest treasure is our self-respect...
yet too often it remains buried within us...
Re-discovering this treasure involves serving yourself first.
That does not mean taking first...
It means putting yourself in order first.

For CEOs that translates to:
Knowing why you value what is really important to you;
Knowing that your actions either move you forwards or backwards.

And...
Knowing that The Importance of Self...
has nothing to do with Self-Importance.
The former is valuing and respecting yourself...
The latter is having an inflated opinion of yourself.

Questions to ask are:
Am I really fulfilling my role to the best of my ability?
What inner potential must I release to raise my game?

Because Life is smoother in proportion to the more you value yourself.

Self-Importance has nothing to with The Importance of Self. The former can be defined as an inflated feeling of pride in superiority to others; the latter is about valuing and self-respect.

In life we are each our own CEO with a life-time contract to perform to the best of our ability – that is to seek out opportunities that are conducive to releasing our potential, harnessing our strengths and developing our skills. That is a highly responsible, and important role with expectations to deliver whatever it takes to fulfil our responsibilities, whether providing food and shelter for our nearest and dearest; working all hours to finish what we have started; figuring out how to overcome the challenges that arise, or fulfilling our role to the best of our ability.

Imagine you are at dinner and just as an interesting individual is answering your question, a late arrival interrupts blaming the traffic while checking their mobile for missed messages. How do you feel about the interruption? You had been looking forward to the dinner, were on time and valued the opportunity to speak with the respected individual. What is your respect level for the late arrival?

The real question is: Does the late arrival's actions state that there is little respect for the peer group? Or is it that the late arrival holds little respect for his or her own self? The answer is both as they are closely inter-related.

The point is: we earn respect in direct proportion to the level of our own self-respect. Our greatest treasure is our own self-respect that too often remains buried. When we invest our treasure wisely it influences both our behaviour and actions accordingly. The best way to invest that treasure is to serve our selves first. That does not mean taking first, it means putting our selves in order first. It means knowing:

That your actions move you either towards or away from what you want.
What is really important to you; and why you value it.
That only you can develop what is really important to you.

Aristotle's Law of Expression states: Whatever you express, you impress; whatever you impress, you express. In other words: What you say about yourself, you internalize; what you internalize through your thinking and habits, you display to the world through your behaviour and actions.

2 questions test how much you value and respect yourself:
Am I really fulfilling my role effectively and to the very best of my ability? What potential have I not tapped into that, when I do, will raise my game?

Value and respect go hand in hand. Whatever you do is an expression of you, whether in your professional or personal life. Life becomes easier in direct proportion to the more you value yourself.

19 Fulfilling Needs

The clear and valid definition of business purpose is:
To create a customer.
The customer is the very foundation of a business...
enabling it to exist and provide employment.
It is only because of supplying the customer that...
wealth-producing resources are entrusted to an enterprise.

For a business to become consistently successful...
It must create, serve and retain customers.
Because of this validity...
There are only two basic functions to a business:
Marketing and Innovation.
And in the perception of the customer the differentiator is...
the innovative marketing that makes your business stand out.

The question therefore that every CEO...
and indeed every employee...
must regularly ask is:
How well is our business fulfilling the needs of our customers today?

20 Letting Go

Pulling along a project is different to pushing it.
Think of a chain:
Push and the links go in every direction...
Pull and they align with you.
Pulling on your own demands your resources...
Employing a block and tackle raises everything with ease.
The block and tackle represents an organized system.
Trying to do everything your way results in getting in your own way.
And the harder you push, the further what you want moves away.

When we get out of our own way, we get more done.
The key is to let go of the emotional attachment to the desired outcome...
While focusing on what needs to be done.
Getting out of our own way involves giving up defending...
what we think we know.

This paradigm shift requires consideration as to how you operate.
Accepting that at times we are either...
our best advisor; or our own worst enemy.

Start getting out of your own way and see what happens.

How can you tell when you are getting in your own way?
Thinking that you are the only one capable of doing what must be done.
Defending what you believe is the right way to get something done.
Arguing that your opinion is right.
Finding it hard to let go of something.

There is an Eastern Aphorism: The less you do, the more you achieve, until in doing nothing, you accomplish everything. An example of this simple reality is that after years of experience you accomplish more in less time.

There is a deeper meaning: When we know what it is we want, have made a plan accordingly, and put in place a proven system to make it happen, we develop a clear expectation of what the result will be. However we have no control over the result of what actually will happen – because it lies in the future. We only have command over the process that we expect will deliver the result – because it occupies the present.

The secret is to let go of the emotional attachment to the 'future' result as this interferes with the focused thinking you must apply to the 'present' process.

21 Strengthening Relationships

Board expectations are that a CEO will confidently…
determine, define, share, and then achieve…
agreed targets that benefit all stakeholders.
The secret to getting this done is actually simple…
though hard to get your head around.
It demands a different mind-set:
One that involves being a Chief Marketing Officer as well as CEO…
because the essence of Great Marketing starts at the top.

It's not about signing off bigger budgets…
or advertising campaigns.
It is about inspiring people…
instilling ownership…
growing awareness…
timely targeting…
building relationships and…
following through.

Successful Founders, Entrepreneurs, Business Owners and CEOs…
All have a well-worn Marketing Hat…
Understanding that it is the ultimate key to success.
Marketing must never be viewed as a tool to support sales.
Because it is never a question of how can we sell more.

The questions to ask are:
Who is our customer?
And how can we strengthen our relationship?

22 Choice Words

The words CEOs use communicate…
either strong leadership…
or poor command.
Choosing, for example:
"Fascinated by this interesting challenge"
In preference to:
"Worried by this frustrating problem"
Instantly transforms negative energy into a positive intensity.

Words bring out emotions:
They make us laugh and cry…
They can inspire, frighten, heal or wound.
We are motivated when we hear them in powerful speeches…
Yet threatened when we hear them carry negative connotations.
Choosing the right words generates the power to inspire, command…
and resolve every situation faced.
Consider, for example, the following choice of words:
Furious or Passionate
Irritated or Stimulated
Impatient or Anticipating
Stupid or Unwise
Insecure or Questioning
Anxious or Expectant

Be aware that the effect of your words…
will always affect your people.
Because the way you communicate to others…
is the key to effectively fulfilling your role.

At school we're taught to read, write and speak, yet apart from how to listen critically, we are never taught to really communicate. The way in which we communicate influences the quality of our relationships.

Too much communication is done in anger and people who are prone to argue, will claim that any heated intercourse, requires such stimulation. Healthy arguments making for healthy relationships is a myth, however, as when two people allow themselves to become angry towards each other, there are two losers. It is pointless to fight fire with fire, being angry with others burns our valuable psychic body into a charred shell.

The principle for listening is the same as evaluation. You cannot evaluate others until you have mastered evaluating yourself; and you cannot effectively listen externally until you have mastered listening internally.

Through the process of listening to others a high percentage of our hearing is overrun by a constant evaluation of the incoming messages we are receiving:

'What does he think he is doing? Do I agree with this or that? Why are they saying that? Why don't they make their point? What is it that happened to me that is similar? Why doesn't she let me get a word in? That doesn't suit them'. We literally hold two conversations at once.

As our tendency is to listen to others within the boundaries of our own experience, we keep strengthening the root of most communication problems. Because we see the world as we are, not as it is, we find it hard to listen with empathy. Clever listening skills may have taught us to keep quiet while the other person is talking, but most of the time our listening is tuned to something we want to hear, something that is useful to us, or someone we want to impress, sell to or gain something from.

Our conditioning has further taught us to believe that we must get our point in first, particularly during an argument. The way we see it is all *that matters to us. We believe that taking the time to listen to another while not defending, attacking, or judging, conveys acquiescence and agreement with their viewpoint.*

Note how much of time and energy is wasted in some kind of defensive or protective communication, internal squabbling, inter-departmental backbiting, politics and interpersonal disputes. We cannot fail to communicate clearly to another, even without words, particularly when that person is attuned to what is really being communicated. This is because meanings are not found in words, they are found in people. The fact is we communicate more about ourselves in the moment before we speak, than in the ten moments that follow.

What is communicated in the moment before we speak? Trust, confidence, sincerity and compassion; or distrust, nervousness, insincerity or thoughtlessness. When there is trust and confidence we can almost communicate without words. When trust is lacking, communication is exhausting and ineffective. Trust and confidence need to be communicated first; because people don't care how much you know, until they know how much you care.

23 Will Power

Willpower encapsulates our tenacity, steadfastness, determination...
resolution, perseverance, and fortitude...
As the basis of our zeal it counts more towards success than intellect.
Unharnessed Willpower works against us...
as wilfulness: the stubbornness of not doing something...
you are capable of.
Willpower is like a magnetic force...
that transforms us from mediocre to outstanding.
Great CEOs successfully cultivate this force.

There are 3 ingredients to developing this force:
1. Determined Willingness...
Willingness can be lacking when not channelled...
We must be determined to do whatever is necessary.

2. Disciplined Persistence...
Persistence can be futile when undirected...
We must be structured in surmounting all obstacles.

3. Decisive Intent...
Intent can be vague without certainty...
We must be clear on how our choices direct our future.

Determination reinforces Willingness...
Willingness builds discipline...
Discipline galvanises perseverance...
Perseverance supports decisiveness...
Decisiveness strengthens Willpower.

Willpower ignores the odds stacked against you.
Applying this force effectively breaks new boundaries.
Great CEOs lead from the front because…
Willpower made the impossible possible.

_____

_____

_____

_____

_____

_____

_____

_____

_____

_____

_____

_____

_____

_____

_____

_____

_____

_____

_____

24 Responsible Role

The primary purpose of a business is to attract and retain customers.
The primary role of a CEO is to realise a profit whilst doing the above.
The No. 1 responsibility of a CEO…
is to implement Strategic Game-Changers that…
grow the company to the benefit of all stakeholders.

This involves 3 must-do keys:
Placing the consumer at the core of strategy…
Consistently building relationships…
Continuously following through.
This seems simple yet because the simplest things…
are the hardest to do…
Most businesses will misguidedly:
plan revenue before margins,
operations before strategy,
sales before marketing,
and budgets before investment.

The best way to rewind to right reasoning is to remember that…
Reputation is built on…
Relationships that reinforce…
Retention of customers that…
Recommend your business.

We are all prone to misunderstandings, assumptions, hearing half a story and perceiving falsely what we see - the key factors that cause rifts, disputes and breakdown in relationships. Often, wanting the best for those around us, we lecture more than listen, certain that the solution we are providing from our own experience is the best. All of us have experienced regret at things that we have said, and not just those in the heat of the moment. Feeling hurt we have allowed our tongue to cause damage, little realising at the time that the greatest damage is done to ourselves.

Developing long-term relationships involves getting closer to customers, understanding what they want and helping them get it through our service and products. It is providing a helping hand when required. A helping hand, or kind word sown, can never be underestimated for what it can reap.

For example: A poor Scottish crofter, upon hearing the plaintiff cries for help from a young boy, rescued him from a bog. The boy's father, a nobleman, offered to educate the crofter's own son in appreciation. In time the Scotsman's son graduated from St Mary's Hospital Medical School, London. He later became Sir Alexander Fleming, the discoverer of penicillin. Years later, the nobleman's own son was stricken with pneumonia and would have died were it not for the use of penicillin. The nobleman was Lord Randolph Churchill and his son was Winston Churchill, one of the twentieth century's greatest leaders.

None of us can ever begin to imagine how holding out a helping hand towards another can either directly or indirectly influence the future success of our business or indeed affect the destiny of Mankind. Conversely, we can never imagine what we are taking away from someone because of either a thoughtless word or through lack of praise.

Couples and partners that stay together are those who have come to respect and accept each other because there is giving and receiving in harmonious proportions. That is the basis of all successful relationships, partnerships and alliances. There must be mutual recognition of what the other needs and brings. Each party sustains the other.

The quality of our lives is reflected in the quality of our relationships. They provide the fundamental environment for our growth, experiences and character, and it is important to choose to reap strong relationships. The degree of pain we feel is in direct proportion to how weak our relationships are. When those that are important to us are strong, we feel secure; when they are not, we feel insecure. Every relationship we embark upon requires risk, but the greatest risk is trying to be the person we feel we ought to be, instead of what we are.

25 Constant Change

19th Century companies disappeared through fixed thinking…
20th Century companies followed in unison…
21st Century companies will continue to disappear…
each citing Economy, Debt, Management, Markets, Overheads…
Banks, Government and new technology…
blaming any reason other than accepting the simple truth:
That Change is Constant.

Darwinism is not about survival of the fittest…
It's about the thriving of the most adaptable to change.
90% of companies operating in the 19th Railway Industry disappeared…
The ones that thrived continue to operate in their real industry:
'Customer Service Communications'

Have you identified the industry your business is really in?
The answer is not easy, but knowledge of it makes the difference.
It is pointless to say:
"We just have to weather the storm"
Yet storms bring down old structures…
Ensuring that unprepared companies will always be blown away.

What to do?
Be canny, ready and agile for entering tight doors to the unknown…
prepared for when those wide-open doors, so familiar to you…
inevitably shut.
Review the energy levels in your team because…

Fixed thinking focuses on what you *can't* do…
in which case the energy is low.
Agile thinking focuses on what you *can* do…
in which case the energy is high.

26 Vital Few

Leadership expects strategic vision...
Management involves operational diligence...
Business demands consistency and excellence.
Delaying what is important due to indecision then becomes urgent.
A well-run business does not have 'urgent'...
unless there is an emergency...
When things are done when they should be done...
how can they become urgent?

What must be done?
1. Acknowledge that every distraction from your focus...
is because you choose to allow it.
2. That advance planning is invaluable...
and dormant plans are worthless.
3. List important items at the end of each day for the following day...
and keep it below 7 items...

Any more than 7 and you are either...
occupying your time with 'urgent' or not delegating enough.

Using the analogy of making a movie, a CEO's role must be one of director – not producer, editor, camera, casting, make-up, stunt-driver, dolly-grip, gaffer, carpenter, and a thousand others all of which WANT and DESERVE credit, because their role – however small – was still important to you, as Director in making the film and to every movie-lover enjoying the film.

As a Director your role is to know how you want your movie to appear AND you want it to be successful, profitable, reputable, and worthwhile. Now your role might well include being writer, director, producer and camera and in doing so you may choose to make just one movie every 10 years like James Cameron. Yet the credits on both Titanic and Avatar were still some of the longest ever as so many tasks were outsourced and delegated. You can be sure that Cameron did not do errands.

Delegating does not mean finding someone like you, to do your role. Artists, Celebrities, Musicians, Writers, Athletes, Film Directors cannot delegate their role either – as people want a piece of them, either their skill or fame. It means finding someone that is much better at doing what you are not good at doing.

To Delegate effectively make sure you…

1. Choose the right delegate worth teaching and delegating to.
2. Define exactly what it is you want doing.
3. Explain why it is to be done, how and when you want it done.
4. Teach the person so that they are sure and then check their results.
5. Expect a regular update and irregularly inspect progress.
6. Appraise, Praise and Raise as required: Recognition works.
7. Beware of credit-seekers that seek power without responsibility.

27 Health Check

Most 'Health-Club Members' stop going within 4-weeks.
Allowing their healthy heart intent to go unmonitored.
The healthy start for a business can quickly go the same way:
Lots of intent with little follow-through.
There are 3 important keys vital to success:
1. Getting Closer to Existing Customers.
2. Resourceful Marketing to Attract Prospective Customers.
3. Providing unexpectedly Valued Service to Retain Customers.
Everyone must consistently and continuously be monitored.

Business is not being active with minutiae.
It is being productive by monitoring what is important:
Fulfilling your Role and Responsibilities professionally.
What does that really mean?

Surgeons involved in an important operation neither...
take calls, texts, check messages or multi-task.
Nor allow interruptions, wastes time, leaves before finishing and...
performs rushed procedures.
Their intent is to follow through while the patient is constantly monitored

Transplant myriad minutiae into idea operating time...
Every new idea stimulates fresh thinking for what you must monitor...
thus ensuring a Healthy Business.

28 Strategic Succession

In the absorbing busyness of leading a company…
Succession Planning is overlooked.
It is strategic decisions…
not market conditions that influence a company's success…
With long-term strategies the key…
is to plan succession with the right team.
In that way unified management teams continue to anticipate future
challenges and apply any course changes required in good time.

Too often a change in leadership leaves a void…
in management at critical times…
leading to, metaphorically speaking, the big ship running aground.
This brings no sympathy from jittery markets that pounce on the issue…
and leaves shocked shareholders swallowing hard.

What to do?
The key is to plan the present…
while planning the future succession to sustain growth.
Knowing that strategies will have to be adopted…
and adapted by the team that succeeds you.
Knowing that key executives will depart at critical times…
during any leadership change.
Knowing that it is the future decisions of…
succeeding management that determines sustainable growth.
Knowing that is it up to you to start planning…
your own succession in good time.
Knowing that your own strategic decisions will leave…
a legacy of continuity, not voids.

When you know that strategies will be reliably adopted…
and adapted by others…
and future decisions will continue to positively influence growth…
when you are not around…
or step down in favour of those that follow...
then you actually strengthen your leadership while…
reinforcing the confidence of others.

Strategy is not an operational initiative. The role of strategy is to establish an edge and the strategy of encouraging entrepreneurship establishes a definitive edge that brings greater value to customer and company. Developing corporate entrepreneurship is a strategic decision. Many companies are externally influenced by the competition: imitating, more than strategizing. Leaders thinking strategically must develop the qualities of entrepreneurship. In this way they obtain the edge that outperforms competition. Entrepreneurial CEOs move their business forward strategically seeking, pursuing, creating and then maximising value out of opportunity. To do so they hone certain characteristics.

These are:
Being aware, keeping alert and staying proactive.
Capturing and harnessing the benefits of uncertainty.
Searching for what the market is missing.
Pursuing passionately selected opportunities.
Adapting, adopting, improving, changing and redesigning.
Growing the discipline to follow through.
Focusing specifically yet with flexibility.
Engaging the energies of their entire network.
Becoming enthusiastic communicators.
Accepting that mistakes make progress.

The questions Corporate Entrepreneurs ask are:
What Business are we really in?
Are we clear on our Target Market?
Can we articulate our customer profile?
Does our current database reflect this?
Do we have a compelling message?
How do we communicate what we do?
How can we position ourselves?
What is obvious that we are not seeing?

29 Corporate Entrepreneurship

Every successful business has its origins in entrepreneurship.
Yet the roots of their success are often forgotten...
resulting in a reliance on resources, rather than being resourceful.
Agile businesses are founded by innovative entrepreneurs, and...
Good companies grow under firm leadership.

These attributes rarely exist at the same time...
yet when successfully blended, companies reap the rewards of:
innovative agility and resourceful leadership.
And that's because a strategic edge has been achieved....
Corporate Entrepreneurship.

The excuse: If only we had more resources...
is an anathema to doing good business.
To be clear:
Lack of resources may well be a circumstance...
But lack of resourcefulness is a choice...
With resourcefulness, budgets are not even barriers...
as innovative thinking acted on to stimulate new business...
will always pay dividends.
Make sure your business does not lack resourcefulness...
at a time when it is needed the most.

30 Economic Perspective

Two negatives rife in business are:
Reasoning out why not to do something…
instead of just doing what must be done.
Dissipating our energy worrying about things beyond our control…
we need to get a perspective about our economic woes.
Yes they exist…
yet they are of our own making…
And therefore will be of our own resolution.

We are fortunate to have the opportunity to overcome challenges…
that develop our potential.
Spend a week in a third world country and observe how poverty,
corruption and life-threatening danger is the daily diet of doing business.
Business is the great arena to test our mettle, build courage,
resilience and determination.

We can choose to be warriors of our business…
or worriers easily swept away with current news that carries us nowhere.
Visits to the Business Danger-Zones illustrate…
that the overcoming of daily challenges in doing business…
are vital ingredients to growth.

Hearing gunfire during the night reminded me that Honduras is the most murderous country in the world. With 27% unemployment, 50% of the population below the poverty line, corruption rife, and two murders a day in a city of 330,000, I had elected to come here to meet CEOs that were generating over 7% annual growth.

The visit illustrated the positive attitude that exists among entrepreneurs and business owners in what the west terms third-world countries. Meeting many CEOs during my stay, I asked them if they were at all concerned about the Eurozone crisis that US papers stated was threatening global economic stability. The response was that whatever happened was beyond their control, so they would not waste a moment of thought on it.

I asked if they believed that the next 12-month period would prove to be more economically beneficial for them than the previous 12 months. The response was, "yes of course – it is what keeps us going". I asked: did they blame the government. The response was that they strived to do the best they could, because there was no other alternative. They focused on what they could do, whatever it involved overcoming, because their business was the only thing that promised to make a difference to their lives.

In touring Iran, it is clear that commuters in Tehran are as frustrated as commuters in London. Industrial cities in the south were as worried as UK Manufacturers with lack of Governmental support and heavy bureaucracy. Young people (and half the population is under 25) in Religious cities on the Afghanistan border hold earnest ambitions about their future. CEOs operate under heavy challenges. Most people have two jobs and work a minimum of 12 hours a day to get by. Money is tight and luxury non-existent for most. Without doubt, the reasons for complaining are at a far higher level than in the western world.

We need to get a perspective about our economic woes. Yes they exist. But they are of our own making. And therefore will be of our own resolution. We are lucky to have the opportunity to overcome challenges that develop our potential. Business is a great arena to test our mettle and build courage, resilience and determination. We become the person we are through learning curves: they are the furnaces in which our mettle is tempered into cutting-edge steel. Without them we remain dull iron.

Business provides us the opportunity to focus on what we can do. It is not for causing us to apportion blame because of hurdles that lie ahead. Businesses cease trading every single day in the UK. Nobody starts with that plan in mind, yet seldom does a monitored plan actually exist. But the note of value is that business is about learning from mistakes.

Blame looks backward, whereas responsibility looks forward. The point is to get things into perspective and take the step towards our challenges, whatever they are. To not do so is to place our business in jeopardy – a danger-zone of our own making.

31 Time Life

The key to having more time is very simple…
Wherever you are, make certain you are there…
in both awareness and concentration…
and, whatever you do, be sure of your intent and expectation.
Plan to be wherever you are at any one moment.
Because whenever you are doing what you should be doing…
at the time you are doing it…
you are managing your time - effectively.

Yet what if something urgent or unforeseen arises?
When you attend to what you know is important…
it doesn't become urgent.
As for unforeseen, that is bad timing due to lack of planning…
or awareness.

Time is life: when you don't value time…
you don't value life.
The key to respecting both is to determine how to deal with your time…
and then spend a small daily-time planning accordingly.
The secret to success is getting things done.
Do not spend your time being busy 'doing' things,
instead…
apply yourself to getting done what really must be accomplished.

32 Stop Start

Irrespective of gloomy economic indicators...
A CEO must look to new horizons with renewed confidence.
In business there is one clear goal:
Produce Profitable Results.

There are only 3 Factors that achieve this:
Strategy
Innovation
Marketing
Everything else incurs a cost.
The one fundamental key to increase profit...
that few businesses leverage is:
Strategic Marketing.
The challenge is that most companies market tactically...
instead of strategically...
applying budgeted resources...
rather than creative resourcefulness

What to do?
STOP considering Marketing to be an expense.
START realising Marketing is a vital investment.

Business needs to make a profit and only happy customers recommend.

The customer's version of why your business loses a contract:

1. You did not understand the problem.
2. You proposed the wrong solution.
3. Your cost was way over our budget.
4. What you showed us was not what was proposed.
5. Your people were too pushy.
6. Your price was too high.
7. The results we wanted were not even addressed.
8. We could do the job with our own people for less money in less time.
9. Your people did not understand the requirements.
10. Your people did not do their homework.

What do your people say when they lose?

1. We were outsold.
2. They didn't tell me that was important.
3. Nobody said that was needed.
4. I was never shown or told that.
5. I never even knew they had an internal group that could do the work.
6. I misread who the real decision maker was.
7. I did not know our competitor was in there trying to get the business.
8. Nobody told me how they would award the contract.
9. Must be a communication problem because my contact liked me.
10. It was not my fault.

Clients and customers want to know that:

1. You understand their problem.
2. You know what they want.
3. You have an answer that gets results for them.
4. They feel comfortable knowing they are making the right choice.

There are three main points important to a successful project:

1. It must meet requirements.
2. It must be within budget.
3. It must be on time.

Most people do NOT explain what problems they will fix or how they will fix them. They start out with a background of the company, when it was formed, organization charts, products or services they sell, and locations.

The client only wants to know:
1. *What problems do you solve?*
2. *How do you solve them?*
3. *Do you understand my problem?*
4. *What makes you different?*

You gain credibility when you understand the problem and engage them in confirming or providing additional insight. Then you explain how you will solve their problem and how the result will be measured using the specific criteria you have been given. That is what makes you stand out from the competition.

33 Change Position

There is an elusive factor that transforms an ordinary business…
into an extra-ordinary one.
Very simply, it is a repositioning of where the business stands.
Repositioning itself from *for nerds*…
to *being cool* made Apple the best company ever.
Focusing on *service-delivery* instead of…
selling-pizza propelled Dominos to be most successful in its industry.
Moving from *drink production* for exhausted lorry-drivers to…
life-style marketing for go-getters gave Red Bull…
its wings to global success.
The differentiator *between* being ordinary and extraordinary is…
the former sells goods or services…
whereas the latter is *about* something.

Somewhere, in an entirely unrelated industry to yours…
that has a different agenda to you…
there *already exists* the idea that will reposition you from zero to hero.
Netjets, for example, revolutionised their profits…
after adopting time-sharing from the property industry.

As repositioning leads to revolutionising your profits…
then it is strategically wise to review your current position.
After all, standing for too long in the same place…
impedes your agility.

34
Right Way

Writers research other authors for what is selling.
Businesses browse competitors' websites for a new online look.
Marketers trawl advertisements to emulate.
Producers follow fellow programmers.
Put simply: the crowd follows the crowd:
Convinced that if everyone is doing it…
whatever it is…
then it must be the right thing to do…
yet…
The majority of books remain unread.
The majority of websites are unvisited.
The majority of adverts are ignored.
The majority of programs are boring.

There are 2 things that Corporate Entrepreneurial CEOs know…
1. What everybody else is doing is NEVER the reason for doing anything.
2. Everybody else doing something is the best reason for NOT doing it.

The key is to 'test' that you are not following the Herd by asking questions:
What are you doing because everyone else is doing it?
What are you doing because you have always done it that way?
What are you doing because it conforms to your industry?
What are you doing because your competitors are doing it?
Applying Radical Innovative Strategic Marketing leads you…
to standing-out and becoming out-standing.
Check the direction you are heading.

Not following the herd within your own industry involves looking at other industries and see how their ideas can work for you. In 1928 the first Drive-In Teller Bank Service was opened. Fast food restaurants later copied the drive-in teller service with their Drive-Thru food service. Drive–In Bank Tellers have now been replaced by ATM's, copied in turn from Food Vending machines. Tupperware that built their business on home-based selling simply moved their model side-ways to a TV channel.

Somewhere a company outside of your own industry is using a business model that if you adopted a similar model it would revolutionize your business. Ask: What is successful in another industry that is not yet being done in yours?

35 Having Patience

When patience is fraught we can become annoyed…
with the wrong person...
and say something we later regret.
Getting irritated signals we are running on auxiliary charge.
Aristotle wrote:
'Anyone can become angry - that is easy…
but to be angry with the right person…
to the right degree, at the right time…
for the right purpose and in the right way…
that is not easy.'

The key is to promise yourself that you always save your anger…
until the next day.
Then, if you still feel the same level of annoyance…
ask yourself if it is being directed at the right person.
If it is not, then do something about it…
by asking yourself what is really upsetting you.

If it is directed at the right person…
then address the situation…
at the right time.
Being irritated, annoyed or angry drains our batteries.

What to do?
First, smile at your problems…
and at yourself for getting things out of proportion…
Second, let go your emotional attachment to the outcome…
consider it objectively…

Third, relax in the knowledge that whatever must be done...
is always done best...
when you are re-charged.

36 Marketing Role

An ethos of swift and good has replaced speed and greed…
With marketing aligning once more to business principles:
Marketing is not a support tool for sales and was never intended to be…
It's not about demanding: How can we sell more of what we have?
Its real role is to ask: Who is our customer?

It's not about spending huge budgets to build media relations…
It's about having customers and ambassadors share your story.
It is not about telling the world what your company has achieved…
It's about reaching audiences that are attracted by your message.
It is not about irritating questionnaires…
It's about perceiving how they perceive you.

Ultimately it's about building relationships…
With those you are targeting to serve.
The worldwide web is your window to the world:
Customers want authenticity and participation…
They do not want spin and propaganda…
Yet many businesses continue to widely miss the point.
It's about delivering on promise that customers are seeking.
And real attention prompts positive-response.

If marketing is about building good customer relationships it follows that continuous marketing is a prerequisite to business success. Successful corporate entrepreneurial CEOs invest a good percentage of their time on strategic marketing. This is a rarity. Most companies have a marketing budget and then complain that the resource is not delivering any results.

Resourceful Marketing does not cost a fortune. Indeed the old rules of enormous marketing and PR budgets no longer work – much to the chagrin of the wining and dining marketers whose main goal is to secure a major campaign. Millions spent on branding will not deliver as effectively as a strategy specifically designed to make a product or service a profitable success. Peter Drucker made the point that: 'Plans are worthless; planning is invaluable.' To develop a marketing plan or a website as a tick box is missing the point. They need to be reviewed continuously for what is working and what is not working. Keep reviewing and planning until it delivers the positive results anticipated. Then go for it.

Involve every medium within your planning. Tweak everything starting with your headline, your copy, your offer and your guarantee. One inspired idea or word change can make the difference. One outrageous idea can reap millions of free publicity.

When you invest time on your marketing you discover lots of ways that work – ways you previously overlooked. Whatever your business, understand that you are in the business of marketing your product or service. And if you don't think that you are any good at marketing then either get good or delegate to someone that is good. The alternative is to forget about growth.

Do not rely on marketing resource; apply resourceful marketing.

37 Attentive Intent

A little known truth is…
that you communicate more in the moment before you speak…
than you do in the 10 moments that follow.
People observe attention before they notice intention.
A business wins custom through communication…
Any intention to buy is influenced by your attention to customers.

Everyone values attention:
When you pay attention…
you attract interest and…
influence perception positively.

How best to do this?

Listen…
Yes, everyone knows this…
yet are we listening responsively or reactively…
constructively or critically?

More, importantly, do we really pay attention?
Do we, for example, instantly forget the names of…
people we have just been introduced to…
as our attention is elsewhere?
Because that is what we are really communicating:
a lack of attention.
The question to regularly ask therefore is:
Is the attention we communicate…
congruent with our business intention?

38 Bonus Incentives

Perceptions dictate expectations and distort communications.
Airlines have passengers and Banks have borrowers…
Yet the reality is that both must have customers.
Customers provide revenue and profit that ultimately fund bonuses:
Those additional rewards received for exemplary work.

All of us respond to incentives…
Most of us value the recognition that bonuses represent…
Some industries perceive bonuses as a rightful remuneration…
Yet we must never view them as a cultural right.
Bonuses must be an incentive to excel…
Inline with strategic ambitions and reputation…
and customers' perceptions and your relationship with them.
They are not to keep someone from leaving.
When you do that, you must ask:
What message are you communicating?

The best form of advertising, building your reputation and making a business profitable is by 'good' word of mouth. The publishing phenomenon of Harry Potter was built this way. The best competitive advantage any business has, to develop solely on its own, is its customer and employee relations. They form the essence of any message you are communicating.

We all share countless experiences of being delivered surly service by people that don't like what they are doing, don't know what they are doing. If we do not train our people they will not improve and never know the best way to provide a service.

Customer and Employee relations are vital. Both customers and employees only want one thing – the same thing as you. Value. They want to feel valued, be valued and receive value. Think of your best customers. Their names will come to mind quickly because they generate a good income for you. Indeed many people are more concerned what they will do if they lose that customer.

Now ask yourself if you know what that customer's mission and goals are. What their values are and what they stand for. If you do not know these basic questions, then ask yourself if you are really valuing them – or just perceiving them as a transaction.

Take long customer surveys for example. No one likes to fill them out - yet countless businesses develop them and send them to their customers.

There are only ever 3 questions required to ask of a customer.

What are we doing that you would like us to stop doing?
What are we doing that you would like us to do more of?
Will you be willing to recommend us?
The first 2 questions relate to improving your service. It is question 3, however that is the key to growth – because it is asking if the customer is a 'word-of-mouth ambassador.'

The value of a loyal customer happy to be an ambassador for a business is immeasurable. When a customer contacts your business, they are, as far as they perceive it, contacting one of your ambassadors – not an employee. Whoever they speak to, as far as that customer is concerned, represents the business. That is why employees must become your first ambassadors. Like any good ambassador, people must be absolutely sure about what they do and why they do it. They are the catalysts for turning every one of your one-time customers that choose to buy from you, into lifetime customers.

Instigating a plan to motivate your people to become ambassadors and reward your customers bonuses for excelling at being ambassadors that wins business and raises reputation is the start to building your business phenomenon.

39
Majestic Leadership

60 Years as CEO of The Royal Family Firm is a unique achievement.
To attend 370 engagements a year even at age of 86 is unprecedented.
To do so every year demands commitment, discipline, acceptance…
and love for one's duty:
Surely the attributes of a True Professional Human Being.

Business today needs true leaders that value…
instinct and intuition, as well as analysis and rationality…
who can be tough, yet tender; focused yet friendly…
and lead their companies in the right direction every time.

2 Millennia ago Lucius Seneca wrote:
"It is not because things are difficult that we do not dare…
it is because we do not dare that they are difficult."

We must commit ourselves to accepting that…
whatever adversity or circumstance we encounter…
it is the decisions we make and the actions we take…
in responding to these events that control us…
it is not the events themselves.

It is our responsibility to constantly improve ourselves…
and influence others by our example.
The Queen's example is one essential for a company's legacy.

40 Firmly Fair

Seasoned founders and CEO's accept an important truth:
They are responsible for the success or failure of their business.
Success requires the support of others:
Yet there are 3 types of others:
1. Those that work for you.
2. Those that work with you
3. Those that work against you.
A good team of loyal people is rare...
difficult to develop, yet essential for success.
Therefore a good leader must be tough yet tender...
firm yet fair.

Striking a balance between severity and leniency...
authority and kindness...
reprimand and praise...
makes for a good CEO.

Put simply:
Too soft and you're taken advantage of.
Too hard and you build barriers.
Be strong and just.

The difference between taking ownership and not-taking ownership is that the former takes responsibility for the success or failure of something, while the latter rationalizes where the responsibility should lie or how to apportion blame. A good CEO has the support of others: A team of loyal people around is essential in the realization of strategic ambitions.

When it comes to developing your people, the people that you rely on and, by law take responsibility for their actions in your business, there is only one way to be in business: To act in the way everyone thinks you are: Strong yet Just. What is the best way to be both Strong and Just? To build a successful business that develops your company and the potential of others? It is to wield an iron fist in a velvet glove. This is the essence of being a CEO: To strike a balance between severity and leniency, authority and kindness and reprimand and praise.

Ikeda Mitsumasa, the 17th Century famous Daimyo (CEO) wrote:
"A leader must be authoritative and kind. If you never exert your authority and are always kind then, just as spoilt children will not learn lessons, your subordinates will not do well. If, however, you constantly exert your authority and are always harsh, you may be successful for a while, but in the long run things will not work out because those under your command will never feel comfortable with you. To have real authority is to treat your subordinates kindly, and to make them feel comfortable with you, but to exercise justice so that laws are respected. If you are never lenient, your authority will lose its force, and if you are never severe, your kindness will become ineffective."

Striking the right balance takes time but while learning lean towards being firm before fair, because ultimately the buck stops with you. Above all do not be taken advantage of. When people take advantage of you, you lose.

To wield an Iron Fist in Velvet Glove:

1. Apply rigorous standards when training your people.
2. Surround yourself with the right people and develop a good team.
3. Be the one that sets the right targets for your team to follow.
4. Make use of the abilities of others and not just rely on your own.
5. Address head-on every challenge that undermines your company.
6. Do not hold back from giving praise whenever it is deserved.
7. Take firm decisions and ensure your people keep to them.
8. Recognize that the key to success is all out effort by your team.
9. Be objective in matters of hiring your people and team.
10. Be respected and accepted by your people.

41 Silent Listen

Too often we are defensive about our actions…
and offensive with our criticisms.
Imagine applying a communicative axiom to everyone you meet of:
Never defend your actions; never attack another's.

Most people rarely remain silent and seldom listen properly…
feigning attention whilst compiling what they want to say.
There is a simple powerful truth to guide us:
The words SILENT and LISTEN are anagrams of each other;
because they always work as a team.
You cannot do one without the other.

When we really Listen we must be Silent…
even if we have to wait to consider a reply.
Without being Silent we neither hear ourselves think…
nor Listen to what others are saying.

To truly listen to another involves emptying ourselves of…
our assumptions and prejudices.
In this way we appreciate where others are coming from.
Because the real secret to good communication is:
Making others feel valued.

42 Specialist Strategy

The best way for the world to seek you out is…
to be the very best at what you can do.
That's the essence of being an expert in your field.
It is not about academic qualifications or having the right certification…
It is not about impressing your peers…
It is about impressing your clients…
It is about building the reputation that you deliver the best.

One hour a day studying your subject keeps you up to date and sharp…
and asking what your clients and customers really, really want.
Then figure out the best way to deliver it to them.
People prefer specialists.
Specialists do not encounter price resistance…
because the value delivered is measurable and significant.
Becoming the winning gladiator in your business arena…
is a strategy that benefits your customers, your company and your future.

When you authentically express yourself, the world embraces the enthusiasm and commitment you display. It applauds your individuality. The key is to find out what you are good at and to specialise in it. Those that specialise enjoy rewards that are disproportionate from average.

Specialisation is the most important factor in evolution itself. Every species has a tendency to seek out its ecological calling and develops its strengths accordingly in order to fulfil itself. Management, however, has a tendency to be influenced by artificial circumstances rather than natural conditions, thus seeking to adapt and improvise rather than create and develop.

A company that has evolved because of its speciality, for example, may later become concerned about changing markets or competition and consequently diversify. Instead of reviewing core skills and adapting them to meet the changing demands of the marketplace, it gets involved in areas that are not conducive to its strengths. Where it was once in command, it is now adversely influenced by fluctuations beyond its control.

To specialise does not mean to restrict the possible range of services or products, so long as they are complementary. Where a law firm may choose to cater for every eventuality, an individual lawyer who does so will be mediocre. Where a mediocre lawyer mistakes being busy for being successful, a specialist lawyer is in demand irrespective of fee. Indeed, regardless of the business, when you are competing with a specialist, your profitability will be determined by the service they offer against yours.

Specialist knowledge is critical for attaining leadership irrespective of the marketplace. Knowledge provides the edge in specialisation to the extent that if you are not continually learning in your specific subject, then whenever you meet another person who is, they will win, and you won't.

43 Winning Edge

A group of CEOs from diverse industries were asked…
Do you expect your business to grow next year?
The unanimous response was yes.
When asked: 'what strategy will give you the edge you want?'
The varied responses ranged from:
More deals, more sales and more customers…
to cost efficiency and better budgeting.
All these are operational initiatives, not strategies.

To be clear…
Strategy is not a vision or mission statement.
Strategy is not goals, budgets or business plans…
these are about implementation.
Strategy is not Data Analysis.
Strategy involves making decisions about…
Where resources must be concentrated.
Who to target as customers and not to target…
What products or services to offer and…
how to undertake activities efficiently.

The essence of Strategy is deciding to do things differently…
To establish an edge that delivers value.
An edge born of a thinking-level that surmounts obstacles…
ignores constraints and leaves the competition standing.
Strategy is about winning…
Start thinking strategically, not operationally.

44 Authenticity

Actions speak louder than words…
Yet majorities lean toward the latter option, because it is easier.
Fighting for what you believe is hard…
Whether a Company Vision or a Democratic Opinion…
both involve much more than talk or ticking a box.

On average 30% of an electorate with the right to vote…
take action to voice their choice of leadership.
The 70% majority prefer complacency to commitment.
Complacency is procrastinating without a conscience…
Put simply: doing less than required.

Commitment is something you discover deep inside…
after you align what you do with what you believe in.
It is not something you manufacture…
It is much more than talk…
It is doing whatever it takes.

Getting enough boxes ticked may suffice for politics
But Authentic Leadership in Business demands much more…
It is sharing a sparkling vision that ignites everyone's involvement…
because such involvement is the kindling of commitment.
Under such commitment words always transform into action.

The authentic CEO does not lead for the sake of money or praise, yet receives both in abundance.

The authentic CEO does not pretend to be special as he or she knows that no one person is better than the rest of humanity.

The authentic CEO is principle-centred and not self-centred and uses the minimum of force to act effectively.

The authentic CEO avoids egocentricity and emphasizes being rather than doing.

The authentic CEO has a light touch, is not heavy handed, will neither attack nor defend, and will know to look at both sides of any situation.

The authentic CEO pays equal attention to all disputes and is aware of prejudices in judgement.

The authentic CEO looks to what is happening rather than what might be happening and isn't. By being more aware of what is actually happening this leader can do less yet achieve more.

The authentic CEO does not indulge in faking knowledge but says: 'I don't know'.

The authentic CEO knows that the reward for doing the work rises out of the work.

45 Objectivity

Whenever we return from recreational pleasures to matters of work…
it is worth considering that…
if we carry on doing what we have always done…
then we will carry on getting what we have always got.
Most good intentions to see things differently…
resemble poor-preparation for hurdles ahead:
Hitting the first barrier we retreat to our comfort zone…
where we continue with what we have always done…
in the bizarre hope that we might obtain a different result.

What to do?
To see and do things differently:
Be radical in how you look at what you do.
Ask someone important to you, perhaps your best customers…
to be objective about your business…
You can only ever be subjective about what you do…
because you are too close to it.

An objective appraisal by another…
will stimulate you to do things differently.
And when you can do that…
things happen for the better.

46 Role Clarification

We are not responsible for others' irresponsibility…
yet we are responsible for whether we succeed or fail.
There are 3 key responsibilities essential for business leaders:
To develop a worthy vision that inspires passion and commitment.
To make a profitable return.
To determine, define and deploy our role as the driving force.

Key individuals must also be clear about their role and responsibilities.
Termination happens because the role had not been fulfilled as expected.
Getting the right people in the right role with the right understanding…
is a two-way street:
When a detailed clarification of their role is not forthcoming...
Then incoming key people must determine and define it for themselves.
Performing on the basis: 'let's see how it goes' incurs a shoddy start…
The route of misguided expectations and misunderstandings.
Most job insecurity is directly related to lack of role clarification.

It is fundamental to good business that people are clear about their role and responsibilities at commencement. Almost always the termination of a position is because the role had not been fulfilled as expected. People must understand what it is they have to do and what is expected of them.

It is vitally important to get the right people in the right role with the right understanding at the outset and this is a two-way street. An incoming executive must expect a detailed clarification of their expected role and also prepare a detailed brief on their own and ensure that all appropriate persons are made aware of it.

Developing a detailed document of duties does not mean replacing flexibility with rigidity. That is just an excuse for not having one, because such a detailed brief should include primary, secondary and additional expectations.

Ernest Shackleton, the explorer, made it clear that in addition to his men's specific roles within an expedition, there was the expectation to help with all general work and whatever was required in an emergency. That said, even with all the uncertainly of what lay ahead, Shackleton provided written briefs detailing exactly their duties and what he expected from each of his crew. He knew that most work relationships fail because of misunderstandings and lack of communicating.

Every person connected with a business either increases or decreases profitability. Some people may have no visible effect on profits, but no effect actually translates into a loss because business is about making profit, not treading water. Everyone must know what is expected of them. Recruiting, developing and retaining the right people demands establishing this at the outset; and starting as you mean for them to continue.

Most families know their roles because of high communication. It is, of course, relatively easy to maintain a family-like atmosphere when a company is small. As the number of personnel increases, however, a *corporation tends toward bureaucratization and human relations grow formalized. Most job insecurity is related to lack of role clarification.*

Questions to ask are:

1. Have we determined, defined, and clarified what we do?
2. Are we able to articulate, communicate and duplicate it concisely?
3. Have we established our purpose of position and the role required?
4. Do we fully understand our functional responsibilities?
5. Have we defined a plan with expectations?
6. Have we agreed a strategy for fulfilling our role and responsibilities?
7. Do we review our plan, expectations and strategy – regularly?
8. Do we understand what motivates us?

47

S.I.M. Card

Strategy…
Innovation…
Marketing…
The 3 contributory factors that stimulate growth…
EVERYTHING else incurs a cost.
Many businesses are too busy to innovate…
or implement winning strategies with radical marketing campaigns.
No surprise therefore that resulting growth is single digit or non-existent.

What must be done to change this?
Where plans soon become obsolete…
planning itself is invaluable

So, in planning your objectives, make sure you…
Refine and align your operational attention with Strategic intention…
Take action to stimulate and generate resourceful Innovation…

Take time to determine and implement targeted Marketing…
Inserting a powerful New S.I.M. Card of:
Strategy, Innovation and Marketing…
Stimulates the contributory Game-Changer for future growth.

48

T.E.A.M. Value

There is only one reason a company will employ someone:
To add value…
in measurable percentage terms.
Those that do so improve the company…
those that don't impede the business.
The secret to effective employer-employee communication is…
making people feel valued.
The secret to good teamwork involves…
commitment and communication.

It's not that people are wrong…
it is that teams are wrongly put together.
A good team is greater than the sum of the individual members:
Everyone must be chosen because of his or her strengths…
and diverse thinking that complements other members.
A common understanding for a team's existence is that:
Together Everyone Achieves More.
Hiring the right people for this right T.E.A.M. is key.

Traditional interviews do not always give guidance as to what value a person will bring and whether they will be the right person for a team. You cannot rely on curriculum vitae. You want to know that a person has the right motives and will achieve what is required. Character and disposition are not discovered in career resumes or in constricting application forms.

Questions on competency and experience will not ascertain whether someone shares your vision. Therefore when identifying the right people it is important to develop a clear mental model of the successful candidate. Know exactly the sort of person you are looking for. There are certain characteristics to identify in fostering the right people. You may not find them all but you should expect more than less, otherwise keep looking. To get what I have termed the right: C.O.D.E:

Chemistry: *You will enjoy working with that person.*
Optimism: *They will lift the spirit of your business.*
Dedication: *They will help towards achieving your mission.*
Enthusiasm: *That will grow into a passion for what they do.*

Additional characteristics include:
Compatibility: *That will ensure harmony and team strength.*
Character: *A fearlessness to do what ever it takes.*
Loyalty: *To work alongside you through thick and thin.*
Humorous: *The ability to keep things in perspective.*
Industrious: *An abundance of physical and mental energy.*
Desire: *Their energy is fuelled from their commitment.*

Ask questions to get to know the real person. For example:
1. *If you were financially independent what would you do?*
2. *What do you hope to be doing in five years from now?*
3. *What is the biggest risk you have ever taken?*
4. *What movie part would you most like to play?*
5. *What was the last/best book you read?*
6. *What TV shows do you like to watch?*
7. *What is your favourite recreation?*

8. What music do you like?
9. What five words do others use when describing you?
10. Why do you want to work here?

Continuous development with reward and recognition are essential for a motivated and effective team. Right teamwork involves hard work and commitment from every member. In this way, trust and mutual respect are simultaneously strengthened and mistakes are openly discussed and viewed as an opportunity to learn and grow. It is not that people are wrong; it is that teams are wrongly put together.

Questions to ask are:
1. Are you a part of an effective team?
2. Does your team know its purpose?
3. Are you a good team member?
4. Does your team generate innovative ideas?
5. How would you describe your team's spirit?
6. Has your team got the right people?
7. Do the members know their roles?
8. Have all members got the right attitude?
9. Is the communication good?
10. Does your team follow through?

The responsibility for having the wrong member and a poor team member is yours. Address the situation without delay, as the problem will not go away. Accept that you made a mistake and choose again.

49 Motives

The right motives are more important than the right moves…
The simple key is to know what you stand for.
When you know what you stand for…
the right moves naturally follow.
When we don't know what we stand for…
we will fall for anything.
Understanding our motivation…
Not only from the commercial aspect…
Guides us to do the right things – not just do things right.

The difference between getting by and getting on is an inner drive.
That fuels that extra mile of commitment.
Commitment does not come from external influence…
it is born from internal motivation…
knowing the reasons why something is important to you.

Re-assess your motives for why you do what you do.
What sort of a difference are you making?
Do you want your people motivated only by:
what's in it for me?
If you think about it, people don't die from hard work…
They die from hard work they hate.
In our 24-hour society, when the going gets tough…
the tough are more motivated.
Knowing what you stand for motivates you…
then the right moves naturally follow.

50
Review Redirect

Agile entrepreneurs found companies...
and corporate leaders ensure sustainable growth.
Corporate Entrepreneurial Leaders have:
Insight for what the future will be;
Intuition for making right decisions;
Initiative for taking ownership;
Innovation for creating differently;
Integrity for following through correctly.

Re-instilling the spirit of entrepreneurship into corporate
management…
reassures stakeholders…
re-energizes leaders…
and revitalizes talent.

Why not…
Review how you go to market ensuring it feels authentic yet innovative…
Revisit your strengths: why do your best customers return to you…
Redirect your business to where you wanted it to go when you started.

Successful CEOs share 5 factors in common.

PRODUCE A PROFIT
A CEO is absolutely clear that it is their responsibility to Produce Profitable Results. Understanding that a business must attract and retain customers they embrace the responsibility that they have to figure out every possible way to achieve this purpose while making a healthy profit. Because a business without customers can never be healthy and inevitably leads to adopting a policy of attracting more loans to keep going, instead of focusing on a strategy of creating more customers to keep growing.

THINK STRATEGICALLY
It is the role of a CEO to think strategically and how strategic ideas can be transformed into double-digit profit. It is not the role of a CEO to think operationally. The role of strategy is to establish a definitive edge that will deliver value, profitable return and leave the competition standing. Entrepreneurial Leadership, which is the blending of those agile attributes instrumental in the successful founding of a company with the leadership skills required to sustain profitable growth, introduces a definitive edge that delivers greater value to both customer and organisation. The key is to refine and align Operational Attention with Strategic Intention.

KEEP FOCUS
Successful CEOs do not allow distractions. And they know when to say no. Business is not being active with minutiae. It is productively getting done what is important. Successful CEOs get things done. And herein lies the challenge, for most CEOs may want their people to get things done, yet repeatedly ask about the 'doing' of what they want done. Of the 3 stages of important work: Do, Doing and Done, only the last is actual accomplishment. And to accomplish great things, there is a clear discipline to ignore distractions.

BE RESOURCEFUL

Being resourceful when resources are low. Too often the excuse is: If only we had more resources…or… we haven't got the budget. If we did we could then initiate the plans we would like. Actually this is more than an excuse: It is procrastinating about what must be done and certainly an anathema to doing good business. The real problem in business is a lack of resourcefulness. With resourcefulness, actual resources and budgets are not even barriers, as resourceful innovative thinking stimulates new business that generates more profit.

CONCENTRATE COMMITMENT

The fifth element is commitment to continue doing whatever is required even after the motivation has left you. It is only tough times that test commitment and prompt CEOs to take misguided actions. When funds are low, there is a tendency in business to seek out anyone and everyone to market your product or service to. But your product or service will never please everyone. Do not dilute the value of your product or service and your commitment. The key is to re-clarify exactly 'who' is your customer and 'what' is your market… and then to figure out ALL the best ways to attract, deliver to, and retain that customer in your market.

51 Planning

Most business plans articulate money required and markets desired...
Great plans include profiled, targeted, confirmed customers.
Put simply: a Business Plan without a proven customer is not a plan.
The core purpose of a business is to attract, create...
and retain customers...
and have them refer more customers.
The breath of a business is to figure out...
every-which-way to do that and make a profit in doing so.
The heart of a business is building relationships and following through...
Two beats sadly missed when running to meet budgets.

The common report is: Losses incurred were as expected.
Better to report: Consistent profits were on schedule...
Because: customer + profit = reward + re-investment.
And what makes for that healthy glow in business?
Applying the finger-on-pulse planning...
that delivers more than reliance on a tick-box plan.

52 Hands On

Good leadership is hard to define…
yet easily recognised…
It comes from a blending of character with competence:
what you are and what you can do.
Then you communicate a mission that inspires others.

People want to be led, not managed…
You manage things; leadership inspires people.
Inspiration creates that flash of illumination when everyone says:
'Yes, now I see it'.
Then a vision becomes the shared purpose.

Without the involvement of others a vision remains a dream…
Without willing followers a leader is in name only.
Good leadership is doing whatever must be done…
whenever it must be done.
Leadership is about fortifying our most strategic positions…
This means being involved in the building of our foundations…
our metaphorical trenches.
It does not mean staying in them…
for that would require staying in a rut.
It means hands-on-leadership…
by investing our time, energy and resources effectively when it matters.

A horseman dressed as a civilian observed a unit of battle-weary soldiers digging a trench in a strategically defensive position. The unit leader, making no effort to help, was threatening punishment if the trench was not quickly completed.

'Why don't you help?' enquired the horseman.
'Because I am in charge and these men do as I tell them, but if you feel inclined you are welcome to help them yourself.'

To the unit leader's surprise the stranger dismounted, removed his coat and helped the men finish the trench, then congratulated the men for their work, and approached the unit leader.

'The next time your rank prevents you from supporting your men I will provide a more permanent solution,' said the man as he remounted.

Finally recognizing the horseman as General George Washington, the unit leader felt with shocked realization the lesson he'd just been taught.

First Lord of the Admiralty, Winston Churchill, took responsibility for the disastrous Gallipoli Campaign in the early part of Great War and resigned. Distraught at the loss of so many and determined to regain his tarnished reputation Churchill made use of his military education and went to fight as a battalion commander in the trenches on the Western Front.

Correspondence with his wife shows that his intent in taking up active service was to rehabilitate his reputation, and he continued to exhibit the strength of character of doing whatever-must-be-done, whenever-it must-be-done that had been a hallmark of all his military actions.

Recorded accounts indicate that Churchill was very hands-on, personally courageous, unconventional and sociable - nothing was too much trouble for the former cabinet minister - he trained his men well and they admired and respected him as a leader.

Both Washington and Churchill lived by the same values. Both were active soldiers in war and great leaders during challenging times. Both did whatever was required as a leader. Both were prepared to get down into the trenches and to undertake what they commanded others to do. Could their leadership skills have been better employed in more influential campaigns? The answer is yes and they did.

The time expended by Washington in helping that group digging trenches was well spent as a leader – as leading by example is what a leader should be doing, and the greater the reputation the greater the influence. And, very often, only one time in the metaphorical trenches is all that is required, in which case time and energy are well invested.

Business is about fortifying our most strategic positions. This means being involved in the building of our foundations – our metaphorical trenches. It does not mean staying in them, for that would mean staying in a rut. It means following the example of Washington or Churchill in the building of our foundations, by investing our time, energy and resources the most effectively whenever it matters.

53 Alternative Lines

Unless they are early risers…
discerning diners of a select coastal area…
do not see the local anglers…
each one eager to hook the catch sought by leading restaurants.
One angler arrives first to prepare 10 rods…
resourcefully securing each one in position.

Later, fellow fishers arrive to prepare solitary lines at remaining positions.
All are hopeful…
All have good hooks…
All have the right bait…
yet the fisher with 10 alternative lines rarely leaves empty-handed.
Business must attract customers…
yet most operate with single lines, blunt hooks and wrong bait…
Blaming the economy for lack of resources, and customers.

What to do?
Planning 10 strategic alternatives to achieve objectives is a start…
Involving many platforms to get closer to customers is better than one.
Shifting from traditional, reactive marketing to…
radical, proactive marketing is key:
Winning new business is the result of resourceful, focused strategy.
Make sure your company has not become reliant on routine thinking…
and rigid resources.

54 Execution

The best ideas are worthless unless correctly executed.
Leading CEOs know that with consumer goods:
Strategy is only 10%...
Whereas 90% of success is execution of the strategy.
So here are 4 facts relating to business ideas…
1. A bad idea correctly executed…
is more successful than the good idea poorly executed.
2. Resourceful marketing for an ordinary product reaps greater reward…
than the extra-ordinary product reliant on resources.
3. Thoughtful service is never recommended without correct execution.
4. Without correct execution of your ideas, products or services...
you literally execute your ideas, products and services.
Execute or be executed!

What is the best formulaic strategy for business success?
Great Idea + Resourceful Marketing + Correct Execution +
Planned Service = Reward.

Because with due respect to Victor Hugo:
"There is nothing more powerful than an idea whose time has come"…
and is correctly executed.

It is accepted that just one insight can resolve a hundred hours of hassle, one innovation can take us from zero to hero and just one simple idea at the right time in the right place will generate the profit allowing us to survive, thrive, invest and grow. Application of The 1% Solution that I developed for leading corporations and many schools is a highly effective way to generate and follow through on great ideas. When you apply The 1% Solution you improve the other 99% of your life. Through its experiential application you will discover that it will:

Inspire Creative Thinking
Generate Profitable Ideas
Ensure Effective Meetings
Stimulate Right Decisions
Determine Strategic Direction
Resolve Complex Situations
Cultivate Inventive Innovation

The secret to acquiring the best habits is to not spend too much time consciously thinking about something, but to do so consistently on a regular basis. Our subconscious is always working. When it is reminded daily about something that we want to know, or need to find, it stays on track and delivers for us.

With 1,440 minutes in everyone's day investing just 1% of it either to solve a problem or generate an idea makes good sense and works with significant results. Its acceptance and application is made simple for many individuals as they will either rise earlier or retire later each day, depending on their preference, by the required 14 minutes. Having a 14-minute appointment to concentrate on something galvanises your thinking.

Our subconscious operates 24 hours everyday and it absorbs all opportunities to work for us. Though our imagination is at our disposal too often we habitually use our imagination to dispose of our dreams and ideas. Applying just 1% of a part of the day that suits us best will very quickly build the habit of being creative and resolving problems.

For example, remember the last time you went to bed with a decision weighing heavy on your mind? The result was a restless sleep and you still had the decision to make.

Next time, define in writing exactly the issue; then insert a date in 2-3 days time, coinciding with your chosen 1% Solution period, and then sign it. Only by doing this will you discover that first you sleep well and that second the answer to your question will have come to you in some form or other right on schedule.

This may not happen until you have been applying The 1% Solution for a few weeks, because it takes time to build a new habit. Start building the habit by asking an important question, for example…
Do I continue with this project?
Is this disposal or purchase right for me?
Will this relationship or partnership be for the best?
What strategic game-changer would give us a competitive edge?

The 1% Solution in Business
When The 1% Solution is applied within a team, company or organisation, the effects are multiplied exponentially. With everyone working on a particular solution the power of a collective consciousness is invoked. For example consider a meeting where a problem requiring a solution is unexpectedly added to the agenda. It is proposed, due to time constraints, that a further meeting be scheduled the following week with everyone agreeing to consider various options in the meantime. But no one takes time out to do so until shortly before the next meeting is about to start. Consequently the energy level is low.

Alternatively imagine if everyone had applied The 1% Solution. Each regularly investing around 10-minutes on a daily basis – thus reminding the subconscious to come up with the solution on schedule. Everyone brings positive creative ideas to the table – utterly transforming the energy level of the meeting. Only by practical example can this be experienced.

Innovative-minded CEOs instrumental in founding successful companies have always applied such methods of relaxed-intensity for inspiration. The point is, when you apply regular conscious effort your subconscious, and the collective conscious of your colleagues, actually gravitates towards the solution or opportunity, even if it was right in front of you all along.

The principle behind the concept is simple: when we know what we are looking for, we recognise signals that lead us to it. All of us experience seeing a new word only to come across it again several times within a short time. All of us experience seeing the evidence of something that we have been previously thinking about. The practice itself is common sense because it involves taking the time to do something that works. It is always the little things that make the biggest difference. The 1% Solution positively improves the other 99%.

55 Reaping Reward

The 2 simple truths about business...
is that nothing lasts forever...
and change must be constant.
And that is why it is important to regularly...
Review the way you operate your business...
Revisit the way you go to market...
Reconsider the demand for your services...
Reinforce the strengths that differentiate your business...
Rediscover the entrepreneurial spirit that founded your business...
Re-inspire your people to go that extra mile...
Remind your customers how you make a difference to them...
Redirect your business to where you really want it to go.

Remember that in skidding on ice you focus on where you want to go...
not on where you are sliding.
The truth is that redefining...
re-stating...
re-energizing...
and re-implementing what you and your business are about...
repeatedly reaps reward.

56 Choosing Outcomes

The metaphorical Rome we envision cannot be built in a day…
Yet when we know what we want we want it as soon as possible.
Good business building takes more than just the right motives…
It is about making the right choices and moves…
The ones that take you towards what you want…
and motivate you to keep going, even when times are tough…
because you can start to see results of your efforts.

What of the times when despite right choices, motives, moves…
and effort…
our desired results continue to remain distant?
What is the best action to choose then?
The answer is Daily Practice, Practice and Practice:
Each and every day count toward building…
the foundation of your future success.

Whatever you do that is important to you…
promise yourself to choose to do a little of it every day.
Your power to choose is your ultimate freedom.

Choosing is our greatest power. We have the power to think whatever we choose to allow into our head. Our circumstances are the result of past choices or non-choice. Using our power of choice to make decisions determines our future. Successful people choose to make decisions. Unsuccessful people choose to prevaricate.

When we examine our lives in the light of choices we have made or not made then we can see that we are the person responsible for how we feel. Each of us are the sum total of our choices made to date from our current thinking. It follows that with new thinking and new choices we can decide to be, have or do anything we want for the future.

It is hard to think in new ways. Consider, for example, when learning to drive. There are three pedals but only two feet and getting to grips with letting out the clutch slowly and pushing down the throttle at the same rate as releasing the clutch seemed a real problem when the same foot was needed for the brake. Suddenly, a million mental signals later no thinking is necessary – driving is just second nature. A thought becomes a belief when you've worked on it repeatedly, not when you simply try it once and use your initial inability as the excuse for giving up.

Though we have the freedom in our choice of action we don't have the choice of the consequence. These are always predetermined by the principle of cause and effect where thoughts are causes and conditions are effects. The only way one can make a choice of results or consequence is by making the right choices of actions and attitudes.

Making choices is a talent that must be developed. The more decisions you make the easier it will become to make more, and the more you make the better you will become at making them. To make good decisions you must acquire the habit of making choices and with practice you will become mentally prepared for the consequences and able to anticipate them. Making the right choices and doing what you want are what's necessary to make a success of your life. When we choose we obviously risk losing but we also risk winning. That is why when it comes to our power of choice my motto is:

Right Choice, Right Outcome;
Wrong Choice, Choose Again

57 Cause Effect

A spotlight requires the same energy as a laser…
The latter is simply more focused.
When uncertain about our strategic direction…
we lack focus.
When susceptible to distraction…
we lack concentration
The Law of Focus works with the Law of Concentration:
Where we gravitate towards those conditions…
that match our serious intent.
Both operate under the Law of Cause and Effect
And this is the secret of getting things done.
Where focused concentration is 'The Cause'…
and the resulting expected Condition is 'The Effect'

When we know what it is we really want…
why we want it…
where we have to get to…
and how we are going to do it…
we save countless hours.
Because it is not the hours we put in…
It's what we put in the hours…
that makes the difference.
Far better to develop laser focus than seek out the spotlight.

58 Best Success

The best or worst of times is a state of mind…
UK 1982: Population 46.6M with Zero Cell phones…
Base Rate: 17%; Tax: 60%; Unemployment 3.0M; Opportunity 100%.
UK 2012: Population 62.2M with 65M Cell phones…
Base Rate: 0.5%; Tax 50%; Unemployment 2.0M; Opportunity 100%.
It is your decisions, not conditions that determine your success…
And generally people make the wrong decisions…
For example the majority like to spend…
More on eating than investing in good health.
More on hair-gels than on brain cells.
More on looking hot than on feeling fit and cool.
More on escapist toys than on enjoying life's joys.
Moron being the practice rather than the principle.

Being the best we can be, in everything we do, starts…
with self-government.
To make a difference involves raising our excellence…
to spend our life uninfluenced by external economies or…
domestic politics…
and become the person we already have the potential to be.

Every living creature has the instinct to survive. We have another that sets us apart. It is as natural to us as breathing and can be more important than survival. It is our innate desire to make a difference. Each of us wants to be valued, to have purpose; and we have our success instinct to achieve this.

Why is it that some people lead an ordinary, uneventful existence, others can leave their marks in history and accomplish everything they want? There is little correlation between success and a person's intelligence, education, family background, contacts, appearance or even a dynamic personality. These factors may have some bearing but they are not enough on their own to guarantee success. The majority of truly successful individuals are self-made – ordinary people who set out to achieve extraordinary results. True success has nothing to do with material possessions. It is measured by creative accomplishment.

Most people measure their success as a comparison with others. Yet genuine success is what people do with their own potential, their development and improvement of it, and must be related to their individual objectives. Success defined is:

The Continuous Achievement of Pre-Planned Worthwhile Goals

Success does not actually lie in the achievement of the goal, although that is what the world would have us consider success. It lies in the journey towards the goal: A continuous sequence, or continuum, of achievement.

The point is not so much where we are, but in what direction we are moving. Success is a journey, the result of attitudes and habits acquired en route. It is not the product of unusual talents and abilities. It is learning and application of our talents and abilities.

Goals and objectives must be continuously decided and set. If you set a series of goals and reach all of them then you must set new, higher goals. If you don't you are no longer successful, by definition. You may *have been a success in the past, yet if you no longer have a current objective to attain then you cease to be successful, by definition. Even if you have decided what your goals are, but do not work towards them, then you are not being successful, by definition.*

Finally, if you have set your goals and you are working towards them but they are not meaningful to you, then you are not being successful. Goals must be worthwhile; they must hold meaning and importance to you. The important factor is that any development of your potential is worthwhile.

Success is doing those things that you have not yet done.
It is not a comparison with what others have already done.

Success is more than just the accumulation of wealth.
True success is to be able to spend your life in your own way.

Success has no relation to what you are today,
it's your power to become what you want to be.

59 Ignore Conjecture

Tough times provide a positive stimulus for innovative growth…
Yet problematic periods also feed negative thinking.
The tabloid blame-based news model, for example,
must not be adopted by business.
Conjecture, meaning an opinion or conclusion…
based on incomplete information…
is usually a prelude to blame.
Conveniently forgetting full facts…
must not be replaced by a rallying cry to resign and remorse.

In business good judgement is based on experience…
that in turn is mostly earned from bad judgement.
Developing a culture that is intent on locating blame…
in lieu of seeking solutions, will never be a success story:
because the focus of attention will always be on what can't be done…
rather than what could be achieved.
History records that asking for permission stifles innovation…
the creative key that gives stimulates growth.

So, what to do?
Whenever you really believe what must be done…
then it is far better to go ahead and do it.
Because in the long run, asking for forgiveness…
beats asking for permission.

60 What Counts

Regularly re-considering re-generating revenue requires…
engaging in Resourceful Innovative Marketing.
What does that involve?
It is not spending bigger budgets…
It is not pushing harder for sales…
It is about Building Relationships…the right ones…
And that demands Profiling, Targeting and Timing.
It also about consistently delivering on promise…
And that translates into valuing customers.
Customers are not transactions in a numbers game of:
some will and some won't.
When you value your customers, your revenue targets are met.
When a customer says NO it indicates that…
the timing is not right for them…
they are not your right target market...
or they just don't get your message…
because it is not compelling enough.

Customers dislike feeling that the sale counts more than their purchase.
The secret is to view new sales as tools to acquire new customers…
NOT the other way around.

Recessions are Man-Made and due to the inherent pruning process they act as a catalyst to be the making of Man. Customers will no longer – and should not have to anyway – tolerate over promise and under-delivery. They demand comfort, security and value – and the knowledge that whatever they buy or order will arrive in good order.

They also know that most guarantees are not up to much. Everyone has bought enough gadgetry, whether electronic or appliance to know that filling in a Guarantee form is not made easy. Even at the point of purchase they are cajoled into buying insurance in case what they are buying now will break down – 'in which case it could cost you a lot if you do not have insurance' we are told.

Most companies offering guarantees have missed the point and use them as an opportunity to sell insurance. The fact is that a guarantee can be used as an effective tool for developing business just by using it for what it actually is – a guarantee.

A guarantee should provide comfort and security to someone that buys something – whatever it is. An exceptional guarantee must be developed to use for this and as a marketing tool to encourage more buys. An exceptional guarantee is Nordstrom's in the USA. For many years their New Employee Handbook was a single 5"x8" card containing:

"We're glad to have you with our Company. Our number one goal is to provide outstanding customer service. Set both your personal and professional goals high. We have great confidence in your ability to achieve them. Nordstrom Rules: Rule #1: Use best judgment in all situations. There will be no additional rules. Please feel free to ask your department manager, store manager, or division general manager any question at any time."

There are always people that take advantage of such a guarantee. Nordstom take the view that the majority of their customers have integrity so do not fight the few that take advantage.

Customer service must not be based on the 1% of difficult customers. Most guarantees have small print to get out of paying. The real objective behind a guarantee is to ensure the seller delivers on the promise. It is not to lock the customer in or out. An exceptional guarantee builds trust in your product, service and brand.

Ultimately, that is the secret to building a good business that enjoys sustainable growth. All of us are customers on a daily basis for something. And all of us want reassurance that when we part with our money we are receiving value for it, and will receive the benefits that have been assured will be ours. Most guarantees are formed small print – the type of which we have been conditioned to mistrust. That is why it is such a wise move to leverage them by making a point of them - and standing by them.

61
Right Direction

Research reveals that repeated opinions by one within a group…
will influence direction.
If this means that the loudest voice is taken as majority opinion…
then what's new?
The real danger is heeding the mass opinion adopted by the majority…
because the majority always get it wrong…
The majority struggle with finance and are in debt…
The majority quickly dismiss the ideas of others…
The majority of businesses go bust and the majority say this is normal…
The majority of bank advisors have never run a business…
Yet advise on how much you can have and when you can or…
can't have it…
The majority of advertisers have never advertised with their own money…
There is little point in reviewing a direction if it is following the herd…
Better to turn 180 degrees and go the other way.
Because taking the road less travelled will prove to be the right one.

Greed and Speed, for example, will never replace Invest and Best.
Only through a change in thinking do we evolve.
Without change we continue to reap the same reward: anxiety and
stress. Change is constant; without it we stagnate.
The secret to becoming our very best…
is to make small yet consistent changes in our lives:
to improve our world we must change our self.
The right direction is the road less travelled.

62 Simply Business

Business demands 2 essentials...
Anything else is non-essential.
One is Building Relationships.
The other is Following Through.
Simple yet hard to do.
Too often business illustrates…
management's ability to complicate simplicity...
allowing administrative red-tape to interfere.

Marketing is about Building Relationships – only.
It is not Advertising, Point of Sale Promotions or…
a support tool for sales.
True Service is about Following Through – only.
It is not about securing the deal, add-on costs or…
smoothing the way to get the sale.
It starts with being in business and continues consistently, reliably…
and unexpectedly – because…
Building Relationships and Following Through is rare...
Yet differentiates value-based companies that stand by promises.
The simple truth is that by providing both of these at the same time…
is the very essence of doing business.

Whatever business you are in, when you take the time to build relationships and follow through and provide good feelings and right solutions then it is a combination that unlocks success. Common sense perhaps, yet certainly not common practice, because the fixed-thinking within business is that it cannot be that simple. The conditioned tendency is that if it is too simple, then we must somehow complicate it. Why?

Doing what is 'simple' involves harder work and time than the easier path of complicating the issue. For example, it is harder and more time-consuming to write a one-page concise report than a 20-page document, though the former is easier to understand.

It is harder to answer a question precisely then to be long-winded though the former is clearer. When a colleague delivers a mountain of explanation over a molehill enquiry are you any the wiser, or simply more frustrated?

There are only 24 words in the Pythagorean theorem, 67 in the Archimedes Principle, yet there are almost 29,000 in The European Commission's regulations on the sale of cabbage. Who is going to read the document – the farmer?

As a company grows it seems to influence the propensity to get bogged down in minutiae. Activity becomes more prevalent than productivity. Question routines that start to look more complex than originally intended. Beware of activity that does not build relationships or follows through – it is missing the point of business and the start of complex management systems indicative of busyness.

63 Ps and Qs

There are 12 simple P's to ask Q's of:

Purchasers: The key to having cash flow - How do we attract them?

People: The key to providing service - How do we train them?

Product: The key to customer offerings - How do we improve them?

Professional: The key to reputation - How do we build it?

Planning: The key to effectiveness - How do we measure it?

Preparation: The key to confidence - How do we win it?

Positioning: The key to brand awareness - How do we raise it?

Prioritisation: The key to ignoring distractions - How do we focus?

Process: The key to operational efficiency - How do we manage?

Persistence: The key to going that extra mile - How do we commit?

Profit: The key to continuous growth - How do we margin?

Potential: The key to sustaining innovation - How do we release it?

Minding your P's and Q's is good for growth

64 Seeking Opportunity

Most people refer to entrepreneurs as risk-takers…
entrepreneurs may perceive risk differently…
yet they are actually opportunity focused…
and seek to diminish risk by outsourcing.
Yet, when within an organisation, they are loose cannons…
Ignoring systems and structures that form the company.
Corporate Entrepreneurial CEOs however blend the best of both:
By getting everyone working together to maximize value from opportunity.
They perceive opportunity in everything and anything…
While extracting value to the benefit of all stakeholders.

All around you there is opportunity.
Revisit your offering and develop an alternative perception for it…
What would you do with your product if you were a competitor?
What would you do with your product if you were in a different industry?
Maximise the value of your business by considering all the opportunities…
That is what you are about.
That is what corporate entrepreneurs do.
Entrepreneurship is seeking opportunity…
Corporate entrepreneurship is seeking, capturing…
and maximising the value from opportunity…
But how can we best seek out those opportunities…
that are right for us, and create both value and reward?
Simply look at our business from the outside in…
as an entrepreneur would.

The very raison d'être for entrepreneurship is derived from opportunity. The true meaning of opportunity originates from a time long before modern harbours when a ship had to wait for the full flood tide before it could make it into port. Aware that the cargo in their hold represented the fruit of all their ventures, the whole company aboard ship would be on the look out for the full flood tide that would carry them towards success.

They knew that if they missed it they could lose their fortune to another ship competing for the same market. At the moment the turning of the tide was spotted the cry ob porto would be shouted. Shakespeare aptly wove the implications of winning or losing opportunity when he wrote in his play Julius Caesar:

> There is a tide in the affairs of men,
> Which, taken at the flood, leads on to fortune;
> Omitted, all the voyages of their life
> Are bound in shallows and in miseries.
> On such a full sea are we now afloat;
> And we must take the current when it serves,
> Or lose our ventures.

Entrepreneurship is seeking opportunity; successful entrepreneurship is capturing the value from opportunity; and corporate entrepreneurial thinking is maximising such value. But how can we know what is a good opportunity – one that is right for us and will create both value and reward?

Organisations are confused when, despite their expensive market research and development, they witness smaller or new competitors create value from what would be a perfect opportunity for them. The way a business perceives opportunity influences what they expect to see from their market research. But the main influence is that the models they rely on relate to monitoring recognised markets. They do not monitor unrecognised markets. Established markets may earn revenue, but it is the emerging markets that will create value. And opportunities are about creating value.

The 8 key Points to be aware of in seeking opportunity are:

Opportunity must create and communicate value...
it is not about reducing costs or sales incentives.

Opportunity is more art than science...
when you add complexity to a simple concept you lose it.

Opportunity perceived difficult is overlooked...
few pursue the obvious; many later admit: 'I had that idea!'

Opportunity is perceived differently...
it does not happen by itself, it is always captured.

Opportunity relates to our unconscious seeking...
it follows our interest and experience.

Opportunity asks why and why not...
it is not about thinking how and how not.

Opportunity is abundant; therefore discernment is essential...
we have to know what it is we want and why we want it.

Opportunity is always right in front of our faces...
We must never become so preoccupied as to be unaware of it.

The whole purpose about corporate entrepreneurship is about seeking new opportunity, capturing it and creating and maximizing value out of it. When we select whatever it is we are looking for and proactively pursue it we discover that opportunities relating to it actually find us. The very act of being on the look out for opportunity creates opportunity.

65 Specialization

The important factor in both evolution and business is:
Specialization.
Because every species strives to survive or thrive...
and each has the corresponding strengths to do so.
To specialize does not mean having to restrict services or products...
so long as they are complementary.

Diversifying works best when it harnesses your strengths...
But when it is the result of having to do so…
a business becomes weak.
Where you were once in command…
you become slave to external influences:
because when you diversify, you spread your resources.
When you specialize, you focus your energy.

As Mark Twain advocated and Andrew Carnegie applied...
Put your eggs in the one basket and serve it well.
In that way excellence will hatch, grow and multiply.
The specialist reaps greater reward than the rest.

66 Refocusing

The SWOT analysis should stand for Seek Weaknesses Only Test...
as that is where the focus of attention is consistently applied.
Consider your own habits.
Which come to mind first?

All of us are mediocre at many things...
good at some, excel at few and...
have the ability to become world-class at something.
Strengths are not the opposite of weaknesses.
Like success and failure, or health and illness...
each follows a particular pattern.
Focusing on strengths makes a business stronger;
Focusing on anything else weakens it.
Fixing weaknesses to improve an individual or business is a fallacy.

What to do?
Apply The SOM Analysis for:
Strengths, Opportunities and Merits...
You can revisit weaknesses and threats at a later date...
and discover that they are not as important as you first thought.
Rediscovering what you are good at and doing more of it....
Does not mean ignoring weaknesses...
It means changing your focus of attention.

S.O.M up or S.W.O.T down
There is an obsession for fixing what's wrong. Current business practice is routed in the belief that weakness is the opposite of strength - as illness is to health, failure to success. They are not. Each has its own pattern of behaviour and follows its own particular configuration. Studying weakness will not lead to improving strength.

The common practice of fixing weaknesses to make an individual, a family, team or company, stronger and better does NOT work. It is a practice that creates average and created on the misnomer that if you can identify all the weaknesses in an individual, team or company, you can then dissolve them by developing them into strengths. The principle is clear:

Find Out What You Are Good At And Do More Of It.
Find Out What You Are Not Good At And Don't Do It.

At school we were taught at school to listen critically - for what we don't agree with. Our fine-tuning is on the weaknesses in the argument, to root out weaknesses in ourselves and in others. With S.W.O.T. analysis Strengths, Weaknesses, Opportunities and Threats are reviewed and considered, yet without exception, the categories of weakness takes precedent over what is considered strong. Where is the focus of attention? On weaknesses - our attention easily attracted to what ought to be corrected rather than developed.

Applying the Strengths, Opportunities and Merits analysis, S.O.M. focuses the attention on important elements. In identifying your strengths and focusing on them, your weaknesses become unimportant. Athletes ensure that they only train at what they are good at. In doing so they are remembered for what they can do, rather than what they can't do.

When a company starts out it only has its strengths to focus on. As it company grows its focus of attention shifts towards correcting weaknesses. Similarly parents are delighted about what their young child can do; yet as the child gets older the parents become concerned at what he or she cannot do, focusing attention on the weaker marks in a report.

Focus for 3-weeks on what you and your business really excel at. Do not consider weaknesses or threats. At the end of that period revisit the weaknesses and threats and you will discover that they are not as important as you previously perceived. The point of this exercise is not to ignore weaknesses and threats. It is to change your focus of attention to what you are good at.

Every day we have a certain amount of energy: physical, emotional, mental and psychic, in ascending order of importance, our psychic energy being the most valuable. When our thinking is rooted in improving what's wrong, the majority of our energy is spent in that area. When attention is directed to what we can't do, rather than to what we can do, we unwittingly drain ourselves of our psychic energy. Chastising ourselves mentally for being bad at something, for example, will cause us to feel mentally perplexed, emotionally frustrated and physically tired. Conversely, praising ourselves for excelling at something will cause us to be mentally stimulated, emotionally euphoric and physically energetic.

67

Re-energize

Children laugh an average of 450 times a day...
working adults laugh an average of 15 times a day.
I cannot verify the reliability of this survey...
but I do know that people buy people that radiate enthusiasm...
and we all know that we prefer optimistic news to pessimistic news.
As the latter travels quicker...
No surprise that so many businesses fear the worst.

How can we get back the 435 laughs we have lost each business day?
435 new sales, customers or clients would stimulate that...
But to be realistic...you can implement 5 'R's:

Review the way you go to market and generate demand...
for your services...
in a way that feels authentic and comfortable to you.

Re-inspire yourself with what builds your confidence...
in yourself and your capacity to handle challenges you face.

Revisit your strengths and why you are good at what you do best...
and why your best customers choose to keep revisiting you.

Redirect your business to where you wanted it to go when you started...
(when you skid on ice you focus on where you want to go...
not on where you are being forced to go).

Re-instil the entrepreneurial characteristics that were instrumental…
in the founding of your business and that have been either ignored…
or forgotten over the years.

Picking any of the above will be effective in rediscovering and…
re-energizing you towards receiving those…
rewards that bring a smile to your face.

_____

_____

_____

_____

_____

_____

_____

_____

_____

_____

_____

_____

_____

_____

_____

_____

_____

68 Think Customer

There is a little known business truth...
Profit is the applause for delivering a great performance...
Engaging acts of service that encourage encores.
Profits diminish very quickly through poor service...
Always remember that the 2 key reasons why customers buy are...
because they either seek:
Good Feelings or Right Solutions...

We don't want to be sold mortgages...
we want a home...

We don't want to be sold clothes...
we want to feel good about our appearance...

We don't want to be sold toys...
we want to buy happy moments for our children...

We like buying...
we don't like to be sold to...

And we buy people, not things.
That's what builds customer loyalty.
Genuinely making people feel valued.

Developing customer service
Define markets.
Align strengths.
Think what your customer wants or needs from you.
Then ensure that your business can best meet such wants and needs.
Your customer's perception determines value.
Put yourself in your customer's shoes and ask:

How well do you deliver what you promise?
How often do you do things right the first time?
How often do you do things right on time?
How quickly do you respond to requests for service?
How accessible are you for contact?
How helpful and polite are you?
How well do you speak customer language?
How well do you listen to your customer?
How hard do you think you work at keeping a satisfied customer?
How much confidence do you have in your products and services?
How well do you understand and try to meet special requests?
How would you rate your facilities, products, communications and people?
How would you rate the quality of your competitor's service?
How willing would your customers be to recommend you?
How willing are your customers to buy from you again?
Are you doing anything that annoys your customer?
What are you not doing that annoys your customer?
What do your customers like best about what you do?
How can you better serve your customer?
What parts of your service are most important to your customer?

Consistent performance is what customers want from a service company.
This demands:
Doing what you say you are going to do.
Doing it when you say you are going to do it.
Doing it right the first time.
Getting it done on time.
Inspecting whatever you expect.

Putting yourself in your customer's shoes.
Taking reliable care of your customers is what keeps them coming back.

Forget Selling

People love to buy, but hate to be sold to so forget about selling. Whenever you have contact with the customer, be a true ambassador – because you are the company to that customer. And when you give great service, make your customers subtly aware of what they are getting. The secret to winning and keeping customers is to value, appreciate and thank them. And companies that give excellent service reward their employees for making their customers feel valued and appreciated.

Additional Service Notes:

Integrity in service requires putting customer's interests first.
It is the little things that build a competent, trustworthy reputation.
Do not treat customers as just another transaction to be processed.
Have a service ethos that converts one-time buyers into lifetime customers.
Understand that successful service is founded on personal commitment.
Artificial procedures don't replace attentive, friendly, reliable service.
Think like a self-employed entrepreneur, not a hired hand.
Marketing is about relationship building, not a support tool for selling.

Know the importance of Mission, Values and Customer Service Ethos.
Know that your customers are your greatest assets.
Know that having satisfied customers is the best business strategy.
Know that companies reward their people for giving excellent service.

69 Doing Done

A good habit for business success is getting things done…
Getting things done is accomplishment.
Getting things done on or ahead of schedule is achievement.
And herein lies the challenge for most businesses:
People spend their working hours either 'doing' things…
or planning to 'do' things.

Yet there is a difference between labour pains…
and actually giving birth to an idea.
Successful entrepreneurs get things done.
All CEOs want their people to get things done…
Many repeatedly ask about the 'doing' of what they want done.
People prefer discussing to doing and the doing to the getting it done.

There are 4 stages of important work:
Do, Doing, Delegating, Done.
Only the last is actual accomplishment…
The rest are going through the motions.
Be aware if you lean toward being busy 'doing'…
or are you getting what really must be accomplished, *done*?

70 Time Valued

Too many meetings are time-consuming and unproductive.
Usually because attendees are unprepared:
First in agenda before the meeting...
Second in decisiveness during the meeting; and...
Third, in following through after the meeting.
Fourth in preparing just before the meeting...
even though advance notice had allowed for deeper consideration.
Meetings that 'wing-it' are low in energy...
Voicing considered alternative ideas raise energy.

Make sure the next meeting you arrange has...
A definite purpose...
High expectations from all those involved...
Establishes ownership of action, and...
Follows Through with a conclusive time period.
For a change, place 'Any Other Business' at the top of the agenda...
rename it: 'Any New Business.'
In business the bottom line...
the one that really counts...
benefits when your time is productively invested in doing business...
NOT just proposing it.
If your meetings are already productive, great...
if not, then you need to change them...

Business is not all about having meetings, yet business involves meeting expectations. As success demands exceeding expectations, then meetings must set great expectations.

When you plan a meeting ensure there is a pre-communicated agenda, a specific outcome from the meeting expected, a decisive follow through action understood with agreed ownership and, above all, keep it short. If you spend your business life in lengthy meetings you will have no time for customer marketing to generate profits.

Always be prepared.
Make meetings productive.
Agree follow through.
Beware arranging another meeting on the same issue.
Be proactive not reactive; contributory, not passive.
Ensure every meeting you arrange or attend has a definite purpose, sets high expectations from all those involved, establishes ownership of action and follows through within a conclusive time period.

Place 'any other business' at the top of the agenda. If any element of it is about new business development, discuss it. If any element of it is not, ignore it. Why?

Because any other business that does not relate to new business development and is not already itemized on the agenda should already belong to someone for decision and action. If none of the above is possible then cancel your meeting because your time will be more productive doing real business.

The following disrupting personalities can often be recognised attending meetings. When they do it is worth reminding them that meetings are actual attendance demands full attention.

The Proposal Planner: nominates to have a resolution for another meeting to discuss the possibilities of planning the way forward relating to a proposal that may be worth considering.

The My Way Director: preferring monologue to discussion, though allows group input that can later be blamed, if it goes wrong, yet can take credit for, if it goes right.

The Grazer: arrives either with coffee or starts meetings requesting refreshments as they missed breakfast.

The Cynic: hates every idea with a myriad of reasons why they won't work.

The Late n' Early: arrives late from another meeting and has to leave early to attend another.

The Gadget: continuously viewing electronic messages under the guise of making notes.

Applying The 1% Solution:
1. Absolutely clarify, determine and define the challenge.
2. Clearly articulate & communicate the issue to be resolved.
3. Mutually agree to apply The 1% Solution at an individual level.
5. Set a date and time for a 'Decision-Meeting' within 7 days.
6. Everyone to commit to record all ideas generated – even absurd ones.

71 Competitor Cooperation

3 external levers jumpstart business growth:
OPM is using Other People's Money…
The one applied when requiring investment capital.
The other 2 require no borrowing or investment proposals.
They are:
OPR, harnessing Other People's Resources and…
OPC using Other People's Customers.
Encouraging co-operation between competitors…
and other industries leads to win:win.

When one company recommends customers…
to buy a product from another…
both enjoy profitable return…
and strengthen customer relationships.
Identifying companies that have customer lists…
suited to your own offering is a good investment of your time.
A specific audience that buys from one industry…
will be attracted to your unrelated product…
when buying criteria match your targeted list.

Most customer databases are tired of receiving…
the same offer from the same business.
Another business benefits…
for every customer that buys your product…
while increasing customer loyalty…
because of the recommendation.
Cooperation pays dividends; Competition costs money.

72 Maximum Referral

One of the bad by-products of a challenging economy is…
that people are giving minimum effort…
while expecting to receive maximum return.
90% of all copyrighted music downloads, for example, are pirate copies…
devaluing the creator's product or service.
Sharing fake goods via Social Media is perceived as a favour…
Not paying for something is perceived as canny business.
I have bestsellers in Russia and China…
yet never receive royalties as there are 'no' sales.

Following the 'wanting something for nothing' brigade…
is not a reliable strategy for sustainable growth.
The effective strategy is to decide on the maximum…
you are willing to exchange for a different maximum you want.
To expect the best in return for what you do…
you have to give of your best.

But there is something else too…
You have to choose the customers that…
recognise and appreciate that you are giving your…
maximum in exchange for the maximum custom.
It is better to build a business with a stable of customers that…
value your product or service and recommend it to others.
And herein lies the secret:
Determine who are the ideal buyers of your product or service.
Develop a profile of who they are…
and figure out all the innovative routes to reach out to them.
They in turn will want to tell the world about you in return.

Consider how regularly we support business through recommendation…

I saw that film last night and really enjoyed it – you must go and see it!
Have you eaten at that restaurant yet? – you must go and eat there!
For a new look try my hairdresser – make an appointment!
It's the best book I have read for a long time – you must read it!

We do not expect to receive anything for the recommendations we make to friends – we are simply pleased to do so. Our recommendation even comes with a call to take action.

Most businesses do not have a referral program in place. Expanding your business through referrals is key to increasing customers, raising revenue and improving profits. Introducing customers to your referral program, motivating each of them to introduce one person a year through recommendation could double your customers in 12 months.

The best way to have your customers recommend you on a regular basis is simply to ask them. Again, bizarrely, most businesses dislike asking their customers – under the misguided thinking that they are putting pressure on an important relationship.

People like to be asked and happy to recommend when delighted with your service. That is key: your service or product must be worth recommending.

Going beyond just asking involves developing a referral program. Affiliate programs, for example, when one website recommends the products or services for another website, directing them to that, there is an automatic affiliation reward for doing so. Amazon.com and Google have affiliation programs. Many home businesses rely solely on the income derived from affiliate reward programs.

Often the preferred referral reward is non-cash. Everyone values being valued. If, for example, your favourite restaurant delivered a bottle of wine to your table, in recognition of your regular recommendation that brings new customers, you appreciate it, and feel part of the business. The cost to the restaurant is minimal and new customers to retain are highly valuable. Many restaurants have loyalty programs.

Whatever your business offering, product or service, you must figure out the right reward for existing customers recommending your business. Word of mouth has always been the best form of brand building. Countries have ambassadors committed to represent their country and that very much involves attracting new imports to their country that benefits the economy. Transforming your customers into ambassadors that introduce new customers is about delivering on promise and exceeding expectations and providing motivation through appreciation or reward.

73 Quality Margins

The customer may well be always right but the question to ask is:
Do you have the right customer?
Most businesses operate on acquiring quantity of customers…
over quality of customers.
Thinking a customer is a customer and any customer is good…
is misguided thinking.

One sure way for your business to spiral down is to…
spend budgets acquiring large numbers of low quality customers.
As 'wrong' customers come in you are suckered in to spending more…
to get even more customers to make your return on investment work.
But if the customer is only interested in the bargain you are offering…
rather than the quality you are delivering…
they will depart as soon as they have the bargain…
and they will not value your offering either.

If offering bargains is your business model, then fine.
But a good sustainable business demands high margins…
to grow and invest.
High quality and returning customers will always deliver more…
than poor quality and bargain hunters.
Regularly revisit your quantity v quality business model.

74 New Relativity

There is a New Business Relativity of $E=mc^2$ ...
Where **E**ntrepreneurship = **m**arket & **c**ustomers^2
Irrespective of company age or size today...
future growth is now relative to establishing an entrepreneurial ethos...
with markets and customers.

Non-entrepreneurial-minded companies continue to spend budgets on...
marketing without really listening or following through...
the focus becoming the data, not the market;
and the sale, not the customer.
Marketing is about relationship building; it is not a selling tool.
Entrepreneurship is about creating, implementing, driving...
and following through an innovative idea...
that maximizes value from opportunity.

The reality is that: with customer awareness...
competition intensity...
and less brand loyalty...
bringing the innovative idea to market increasingly fails...
because companies continue to operate under old rules.
The question to ask is: What rules are you operating under?

Non-entrepreneurial-minded organisations spend huge finance budgets on marketing, without really listening. Entrepreneurial-minded ones invest their time, energy and imagination in listening to, and understanding, customers.

The days of 'it's a numbers game'; 'next;' 'love 'em and leave 'em;' 'and there'll be more where they came from,' are over. The marketing textbook adage: that customers know what they want, you just have to supply it – is obsolete. Customers neither want to be treated like a transaction, nor do they know in advance exactly what they want.

A customer-focused ethos involves imagining what the future holds; perceiving how market trends will shift; anticipating what the demand will be; and proactively raising the awareness of customers, thereby actually creating and becoming the future.

Having moved from a product-selling and customer-quantity paradigm to one of customer-serving and being relationship-driven, it is important to know: who the customer you want to serve is; what level of relationship will develop loyalty with you; why they will want to do business with your company; and how you will attract, lead and educate them to raise their expectations and perceptions as to how your product or service will beneficially serve them.

Marketing focus is leaning increasingly inward to existing customers, as opposed to outward strangers. Cultivating and growing a customer base must involve getting to know them well in order to market to them effectively and it is vital that you clarify what market you are entering and establish the customer profile that your market comprises.

There are specifically 15 factors I have identified in order to distinguish the non-entrepreneurial-minded organisation of today from the entrepreneurial-minded organisation of tomorrow in marketing and customer related criteria:

Non-Entrepreneurial	Entrepreneurial
1. Marketing strategy	Customer-focused ethos
2. Market size	Market niche
3. Customer quantity	Customer perception
4. Meet customer needs	Anticipate customer wants
5. Improve service for market	Create service with customer
6. Generalised products	Customised convenience
7. Quality imitation	Desired innovation
8. Customer relationship	Customer partnership
9. Know competitors' strengths	Understand competitors' mistakes
10. External market data	Close customer communication
11. Global scope, local focus	Global identity, personal service
12. Market duration	Speed to market
13. Market leader	Niche diversity
14. Marketing review	Follow-up service
15. Research related	Feedback reflective

Amazon applies entrepreneurial-thinking criteria similar to the above right hand column. CEO Jeff Bezos was more interested in providing a fast, convenient, repeat service than selling cheap books. Being recognised as a valued customer and being offered books that similar purchases have indicated may interest you fulfils customer criteria of speed, convenience and follow-up service. The customer feels a valued partner in deciding what offerings are available. The customer may not be aware of what he or she actually wants to read next, but the follow-up service provides guidance and suggestion on a 'why not go for it' basis, rather than 'why have it' or 'do you really need it?' basis.

It is worth reviewing:
Does your company have a customer- ethos?
Is there clarification of who your customer is?
Has your market been clearly determined?
Are you able to anticipate future niche markets?
Is your customer perceived as a partner?
Does your customer perceive your service as fast and convenience?

75 Life Time

Mobile communications are one of the new wonders of the world…
Yet instant contactability must not demand constant availability.
View any busy street and 3 out of every 5 people will be on the phone.
Observe restaurants and people supposedly enjoying dinner together…
are individually texting.

Being conscious of the moment…
that is: being aware of wherever you are at the time you are there…
is one of the foundation stones to…
relationship building.
Neither business calls from the beach while with the family…
nor family calls from office meetings are conducive…
to building relationships.

We must become commander of our communications…
rather than its controlled slave.
How can we achieve what we really want…
when we are so externally influenced?
When our communications involve building relationships…
and following through…
then the answer is yes.
If not, then they are a distracting waste of time…
And time is another word for life.

76 Seconds First

Our imagination is at our disposal to support our future planning...
Unfortunately too often we use it to dispose of our dreams...
By imagining negative what-if scenarios that sap our courage and resolve.
Allowing a myriad of gloomy factors beyond our control...
to distract us from what we had committed ourselves to do is pointless.

Most of us will accept that what we learn is pointless unless...
we understand, adapt, adopt and apply what we have learned.
Take, for example, having second thoughts...
Second thoughts distract us from implementing the decision that...
our first thoughts prompted us to intuitively make.
Second thoughts strive to be heard through rationalisation.

What do to?
Well, in a perfect world, we would have our second thoughts first...
so that we could then discard them.
The secret is to be clear as to what first thoughts are founded on...
and then to rationalise why we are having second thoughts.

Our minds apply intuition and rationale for apprehension – vehicles to provide a form of understanding. Intuition is defined as immediate apprehension by the mind without reasoning. Rationale is explained as understanding by reasoned explanation.

In rationalising we spend more time inventing impenetrable reasons why it is not even marginally possible to get something, than we do on trying to get it done. In every area of life we have one of two things: reasons or results, excuses or experiences, stories or successes. In the amount of time we give our mind to invent a watertight excuse, we could have created an alternative way of achieving the desired result.

Do not reason why you can't,
Listen intuitively how you can.

Most of the time we are guided by our reasoning faculties – we choose to reason things out, but we develop our intuition by paying attention to it. The key is to use the reasoning and the intuitive parts in teamwork, not competitively. Both are complementary to each other as yin to yang, logic to emotion. The reasoning side helps us to find, clarify, determine and research exactly what we want and by bouncing it off our intuitive side we make a decision and take action.

The reasoning side bounces off the intuitive side, not the other way about. Intuitive solutions are often absurd and by bouncing off the reasoning side they would never become a reality. Picture the person who comes home with a massive problem requiring a decision. All the relevant data has been researched and all the whys and wherefores considered. A brief outline of the subject is discussed with a partner, who comes up with an answer that is seemingly ridiculous at first, yet becomes obvious as the right one.

We allow the situation to arise when our two thought and creative processes are at odds with each other, pushing against each other instead of pulling together. We even misuse our rational mind to the extent of providing irrational reasons. For example the person who says:

I've failed at that once so I'll probably fail at it again is certainly not being rational. To conclude that I can't before even trying something in the absence of contrary evidence is not rational. It is as rational as the people who say they do not like a particular food or drink when they have never tasted it.

Our comfort zone knows us better than anyone and hits us on our Achilles' heel. It uses reasons we find reasonable and rationale we find rational. It takes our greatest aspirations and turns them into excuses for not bothering to aspire. This comfort zone allows rationalisation to take hold during our conditioning years. It gave us comforting reasons for why life didn't go the way it should, for why we experienced failure.

Though our rational mind and rationalisation are essential to our make-up, we must ensure that they work for us and not against us. The rational mind examines and analyses incoming messages and accepts those that are true and rejects those that are not true. Too often we confuse everything with opinions. It is our opinions and the opinions of others that we allow to affect our rational thinking.

Don't let rational thinking battle with intuition by providing reasons why something can't be done. Use your rational mind to provide reasons why they can be done. Dwell upon things as possibilities and don't use the thinking process for thinking of the impossibilities. By dwelling on unfavourable outcomes your mind is occupied with worry. By envisioning a positive outcome your mind is occupied with creative solutions.

77 Apples Oranges

A great idea must be implemented for it to deliver future reward…
Yet too much discussion, too many hurdles, too little time and…
too little budget, together with demands for quick results…
culminate in zero action or project shelving.

Investing time to strategically plan and develop ideas and…
correctly market the innovation is absolute key to future reward.
Strategically Marketed Innovations are what differentiate…
the extraordinary business from an ordinary one:
look at Apple and Orange.

People buy Apple products because they want them…
People use Orange as a network alternative…
and their biggest seller is an iPhone.
Revisit your own ideas, services and products and consider:
Have they truly received the support they are truly worthy of?
It may be simply a case of comparing apples with oranges.

78 Constant Change

There are 3 simple truths in business…
Nothing Lasts Forever…
Change must be a constant…
and the Best Constant is Innovation…
But Inventiveness and Innovation do not of themselves make fortunes…
the secret is in riding the inevitable crest of the wave…
when the innovation becomes irresistible…
and then riding it for all its worth before it peaks.

The video…the DVD…the Player…the iPad have all been irresistible…
and made fortunes during the period they were universally desired.
Fortunes are made during the acceleration period…
before everyone brings alternatives out.
The clear key for sustained growth is therefore constant innovation…
and to make it a daily strategic part of business life…
Though innovative ways of doing things are always initially resisted

What to do?
Transform change resistance into innovation irresistibility.
Innovation is a strategically learned skilled habit…
If you are not constantly innovating, then start learning the habit now…
for there are fortunes in your business waiting to be won.

A successful CEO works hard and puts in long hours. There is a difference, however, between the hours you put in; and what you put in the hours; between what you achieve and the return on your time investment. Putting in extra hours to complete work that does not utilize your time effectively is wasting time.

Say you work 10 hours during a working day. The 80/20 Rule states that 8 hours of your day is 20% productive, while 2 hours is 80% productive. Ergo for 8 hours your time is not used effectively. That leads to fatigue, non-efficiency and burnout. Therefore it is important to know whether you are spending your time on the 80% or investing your time on the 20%.

You are in the 80% if you have to say yes to the following statements:
1. You are working on tasks that are considered urgent.
2. You engage in activity that you are not good at.
3. You are working on projects that you have no interest in.
4. You are working on tasks others have asked you to do for them.
5. You are taking too long over particular tasks and keep returning to them.
6. You find yourself complaining all the time.
7. You work on tasks that do not hold your attention.

You are in the 20% if you can say yes to the following statements:
1. You're engaged in activities that are on your strategic agenda.
2. You have an idea how long a planned task is going to take.
3. You are doing things because you are good at them.
4. You are working on tasks that you don't like yet are important.
5. You invest time delegating tasks to others to do.
6. You delegate the tasks that you are neither good at nor enjoy doing.
7. You are enthusiastic about finishing the tasks you have set yourself.

Everyone knows the value in planning and prioritizing. For every minute invested in planning what needs to be done, you save 10 minutes in the actual execution of what needs to be done. When you plan, the subconscious is aware that you have consciously planned it and immediately starts working behind the scenes on your behalf. That is where linking The 1% Solution with The 80/20 Rule is effective. The questions to help you prioritise are:

Where do I waste my time?
Where do I invest my time most efficiently and effectively?
For example:
Do I have a set time for emails, or do I attend to them as they arrive?

Is my time spent producing, or do I invest it in business development?

How can I reschedule so that 20% of my tasks produce 80% of my results?

How can I eliminate 80% of my interruptions?

By using The 1% Solution – up to 14 minutes a day – to help you apply the 80/20 Rule you will very quickly discover what tasks you should be investing your 20% in to ensure that you produce the 80% of the results you want to achieve. In this way you will be achieving more in less time.

79

Beyond Words

We communicate NOT by what we say…
but how we FEEL about what we say.
This is important to remember because ultimately people buy people…
people exuding passion with integrity: confidence and self-assured belief.
No matter how good a business is…
if you do not enjoy it then what is the point?
If you do not have the passion for what you do…
then either the business suffers - or you will.

People do not die from hard work…
they die from hard work that does not hold their heart.
How you communicate something is more important than what you say.
Each of us buys on emotion before logic and…
metaphorically are stimulated more by the sizzling of the steak…
than the raw steak itself.

The key is authenticity:
Whether composing an email or delivering a presentation…
seek to appeal to people's emotions by being authentic…
because words are often inconsistent and seldom add-up.
It is the meaning behind the words that really counts.

80 Feeling Valued

The final rush to buy loved ones presents for Christmas is similar...
to many companies holding a strategic planning session:
Uncertainty on what to get...where to go...and when to do it.
People browse shops to get ideas...
companies look at what competitors are doing to get ideas.

There is a simple solution for getting it right on both counts:
Get to know what your loved one or customer really wants...
then deliver it in such a thoughtfully packaged fashion...
that they feel valued.
That is the secret to building relationships:
Making others feel valued.

Creating value in your customer's life builds trust:
it is the thoughtfulness that really counts.
A magical moment of thoughtfulness strengthens relationships...
A mean moment of thoughtlessness weakens them.
Ultimately it is these moments of choice that makes a difference

Without exception people who feel genuinely valued will respond positively. Wherever we go and whatever we do, whenever we feel valued, our self-esteem soars – we feel good about ourselves, life in general and, importantly, the interaction we are currently involved with, particularly if it relates to service. No matter how secure others may seem, everyone harbours a little fear of rejection or exploitation. The majority of people it would seem hold a memory that once, during their formative years, they were either last to be picked for a team, ignored or left-out.

Think of those times you entered a restaurant and felt ignored. It may have been because just at that moment it was not physically possible to attend to you – but to remain unacknowledged without even a nod does not feel good. Alternatively, attentive service by a welcoming host who focuses on our requests changes the whole day. It is always the little things that will make us feel valued. Yet always the little things we forget when communicating with others.

When on the phone, you can tell when someone is not paying attention if they are involved with something else. Yet many of us are guilty of doing exactly the same thing. Eating while on the phone is the clear signal of lack of respect.

The action of being placed on hold or transferred from department to department does not marry up with the repeated recorded message of: 'Your call is important to us'. The truth is that though everyone wants to feel valued, only a few situations make us feel so. Questions to ask are:
What it would be like meeting you?
Do you always remember names?
Do you feel unvalued when yours is forgotten?
Are you punctual?
Do you feel devalued when kept waiting?
Making people feel valued is achieved by seven laws of communication.

1.We cannot communicate more than what we are. It follows that being yourself is the key to effective communication. Pleasing everybody by playing appropriate roles is unhealthy communication.

2.Communication is not simply words. We communicate as much, if not more, by our silence as by our speech.

3.Communication must be unconditional. Assumptions, prejudices and opinions must be put aside while truly listening.

4.Communication must be the element of trust that is fundamental to relationships. The lower the trust, the lower the degree of communication.

5.Communication is influenced by perceptions of our beliefs, values and commitments. By questioning our perceptions we can begin to appreciate another's viewpoint.

6.Communication involves listen before speaking. Where the mouth is the mechanism, the ears and eyes are assistants of the heart and mind. When these three respond in harmony, they act in a beneficial way. Listen primarily with eyes and heart and secondarily with ears.

7.Communication requires listening responsively not reactively. Listening constructively not critically: for what you agree, not just what you disagree with, builds rapport.

When you cannot understand another's view don't argue against their perspective, take a moment to step into their shoes to see the view from where they stand.

81 Engaging Dialogue

All of us regularly share a similar experience…
What it is?
Upon entering a store you hear: 'Can I help you?'
You reply: 'Just looking thank you.'
The expected response…
and the end of the conversation.

Better you were welcomed with:
'Have you been here before?'
Eliciting the reply of:
'No', or, 'Yes'.
Dialogue can now continue:
No? – Well, we have a very special offer to welcome first time customers.
Yes? - Then we have a very special offer for returning customers.

Clearly there must be genuine offers in place.
That is not hard to do.
But that is not the point.
Most of us browse - undecided – we like support.
We don't want: 'Can I help you' – that means:
'Can I sell you something.'
We like to buy.
We don't like to be sold.
We like to be valued through dialogue.
We like that.
That is the point.
Inviting dialogue values a customer…
the key ingredient to the business alchemy

That transforms service into gold.
Welcoming enquiries that invite dialogue…
and valuing a customer is what business is about.
If your retail outlets do the minimum…
then you and your customers are both losing out.
If you do not have retail outlets…
then consider adapting the idea for your business.

82 Patient Results

There is a similar correlation between patience and certainty...
as there is between impatience and doubt.
The more impatient you are for something to go the way you want...
the more you begin to question whether it will.
Being patient requires greater confidence...
in what we are working towards.

To build patience...
You view obstacles as opportunities to strengthen...
not indications of failure.

Ask yourself:
1. Are you patient when others do not understand you?
2. Are you patient when the deadline cannot be met?
3. Do you give others your undivided attention?
4. Are you results or process focused in your actions?

Man is unique in placing time constraints on the results that he wants in life and, in doing so, becomes restless, rather than still. It is of course far easier to be patient for something when the outcome of it is certain, because in our certainty, there is less room for anxiety.

The key to being patient is in having greater certainty of the outcome. We each have a choice: Either feeling happy only when things turned out just the way we want; or, feeling happy whether things turned out the way they wanted or not. The obvious choice is the latter, yet most adopt the former.

Consider your involvement with a current important situation.
Think about the outcome you really want. Gauge how you feel.
Patiently detach yourself from the outcome. Gauge how you feel now.
Feel the confidence of certainty that the outcome you want will happen.
Gauge how you feel now.
Notice how concern and feelings of impatience diminish.

Often when we decide we want something, we want it now, and when we do not get it straight away, we feel that life is unfair, that we have been treated unjustly. Sometimes we convince ourselves that it is because others, and even forces beyond us, do not want us to have what we want. In choosing to believe that we have been singled out, we convince ourselves that the acquisition of our desires is at the mercy of the inquisition by others.

We accomplish more immediate results simply through patience. Experiencing it is by far the best way to see the results that it delivers. Persevere and you become aware of things that begin to show up in your life that you have not noticed before. Act on whatever you begin to notice, while trying very hard to release all judgement towards events. Trying to prejudge the result is a sure indication that you are once again becoming attached to the shape of life as it used to be.

To have the virtue of patience, it is important to acknowledge obstacles as opportunities to strengthen you, not as indications of failure. In attempting to patiently let go of an outcome, there will be a tendency to view obstacles that begin to appear as evidence that what you are embarking upon is not working. Detaching yourself from an outcome does not mean giving up on it. Determination and persistence are valuable ingredients in both testing your resolve and surmounting life's inevitable obstacles.

83 Finishing

Success comes about from finishing what you start.
Commitment comes from continuing to do…
whatever is required of you…
even after the motivation that prompted you to start has faded…
Tough times test our commitment…
and prompt us to take misguided actions.
For example, when funds are low…
there is a tendency in business to seek out…
anyone and everyone to…
market your product or service to.

Your product or service will never please everyone…
And selling something that resembles a one-size-fits-all…
dilutes the value of your product or service and your commitment.
The secret is to re-clarify exactly 'who' is your customer…
and 'what' is your market…
and then to figure out ALL the best ways to…
attract and retain that customer in your market,
Raising your efforts and doing even more of whatever is required…
reinforces the commitment to go that extra mile…
and see things through.

84 Sharpening

The veteran Lumberjack was absent from work for 2 days...
This surprised everyone...
because the time lost would adversely reduce his delivery quota.
Good, thought the others, there will be more for us.
The next day, the Lumberjack arrived early...
and cut 2-days quota by midday...
The others, impressed, yet peeved, asked...
"why did you not come in the day before."
"I took time-out to sharpen my axe," came the reply.

The question is: do you?
Taking business to the beach does not re-charge batteries.
To be on call means your business owns you...
and you owe it to your business to be in command.
If you need to stay in touch...
then you must review how you run your life.

The secret is to plan your time in advance...
what you are going to do...
and what you are NOT going to do...
Wherever you are, make sure you are really there...
Then you relax, and start sharpening your own axe.

We all need time to sharpen our axe. Without balance we lose our cutting edge. Nature has a way of telling you to slow up, to have balance in your life. Human beings are the only creatures who do not have balance in their lives unless they create it by choice.

It is very difficult to de-compartmentalise yourself. If you have major difficulties at the office you will tend to take them home with you and if your home life is turbulent you tend to take it to the office. The only way to ensure balance is to have defined goals in all areas of your life.

The discipline of balance can be learned and usually involves giving up something. Children, for example, particularly enjoy the doing of something rather than the setting up of something. They want to get on with it, to enjoy it, and what better way to learn initially. Goals must be compatible and not at cross-purposes for there to be balance. You can't have a goal to take your family on an expensive holiday unless you have financial goals that will provide sufficient income to make saving the money possible.

The idea that we need time off comes from working for another to fulfil another's dreams. When your life is directed towards fulfilling your dream why would you want to take 'time off' from that? Taking time out means nurturing yourself while doing a project. It does not mean not doing the project. Learn to take the pressure off while you do what you do. When you think of recreation, think re-creating your attitude towards the work at hand.

The adage a change is as good as a rest is true. The only recuperative time required is sleeping. Each time you begin to feel stagnant on a particular activity, do something else like learn a language, play football, read a book. Relax with a game of chess. The brain never stops and every time you give it variety the body responds. Balance in life is refreshing.

85 Three Keys

More goals are planned at New Year than at any other time.
Most are soon discarded…
de-motivating the individual.
Goals and diets do not work on positivity alone.
There must be plan of action with clear reward.
Business growth demands one clear goal: Produce Profitable Results.

There are only 3 Factors in Business that produce profitable results:
1. Strategy
2. Innovation
3. Marketing
Everything else produces a cost.

In planning goals have a Business Plan with 3 keys:
1. Targeted Customers.
2. Compelling Marketing.
3. Healthy Profit Margins.
Only these generate growth.
Do not be distracted from doing them.

86 Attention Habit

The key factor overlooked when turning ideas, products or services…
into exceptionally successful ventures is:
Underestimating the attention to detail that must occur each…
and every day.
The challenge is to think in terms of process…
rather than results, while, at the same time…
have a clear expectation of the desired outcome.

For example, zealously taking ownership of what needed to be done…
with obsessive care were the hallmarks of Steve Jobs' leadership…
Consequently he did more to determine how we work and play…
than any person on the planet.

Without daily diligence that must occur every day to be great…
companies limit their achievements.
Becoming obsessive about going that extra mile…
either in preparation or delivery…
is a worthwhile habit not to be underestimated.

Habits are not an instinct they are a reaction. A reaction formed by continually doing something. We all formed habits when we knew far less about life than we know now. Unwittingly we formed habits and they in turn form us. The habits allowed to form years ago end up controlling our lives today. If we don't conquer bad habits, they will eventually conquer us.

A habit is a conditioned response we have programmed into ourselves by continually doing a particular action until it becomes as second nature. To change a habit requires first becoming aware of the habit and the satisfaction derived from it, before replacing it with another that gives greater satisfaction.

Repetitively taking action towards what you want, in place of worrying about what it is you have to do, replaces negative thinking habits for positive ones. For example, take a bucket of water and drop in stones one by one. The fluid representing your bad habits will eventually be displaced leaving a bucketful of positive ones. As new habits force us to react in a manner consistent with what we continually do, we must continue to take action to ensure that our good habits get stronger and our bad habits disappear.

Only by persistently and consistently taking action over and over again will you build up the habit for setting goals. Working on goals automatically brings lots of little successes. Everything you do is measured, achieved and rewarded. The procedure of lots and lots of successes not only builds your confidence, self-esteem and self-worth but it actually creates the habit of success, physically, mentally and emotionally. As habits eventually form us, you will inevitably be a habitual success.

87
Beyond Brief

The accountant doing your tax return satisfactorily…
is doing a job.
The entrepreneurial accountant suggesting creative ways to…
increase your disposable income and thus improve your quality of life…
is providing a service.

The dentist that removes the decayed tooth is…
doing a job.
The entrepreneurial dentist proposing specific restorative methods…
to significantly improve your confidence is providing a service.

The consultant that does exactly what is expected is doing a job...
The entrepreneurial consultant introducing an innovative idea…
to improve revenue and quality is providing a service.

Being a CEO is not doing a job…
The Corporate Entrepreneurial CEO has:
Insight to anticipate future market trends and customer needs; is…
Intuitive in deciding how to act on such trends and needs; acts with…
Initiative to effectively maximise the opportunities that arise; is…
Innovative in creating value from such opportunity; has…
Integrity to ensure such opportunity is worthwhile; and…
Individuality for accepting ownership; with
Interdependence to work with teams to implement ideas.

88 CEO Non-Conformity

The exceptional CEO is a non-conformist…
They are their own person.
That does not mean being unconventional or rebellious.
It is dressing, behaving and acting in the way they feel right.
That is the way they are.
It is having the courage to say 'no' to something…
when the majority say 'yes' to the same thing.

When we see things in a new light, we see our world differently
When we act in a new way, we live differently.
Being our own person requires developing:
Spontaneous Non-Conformity…
Volitional Responsibility…and
Vocational Balance.

These keys broaden horizons…
spark imagination and ignite resourcefulness.

They ensure originality and motivation…
build optimism and encourage enthusiasm.

They guide transformation and right direction…
With confidence and certainty…

In doing so they maintain individuality, strengthen self-reliance
And build self-trust.

With self-trust you are not distracted about opinions…
because you are your own person who…

in the midst of the crowd retains independent thought…
Yet is in tune with the world.

Spontaneity broadens horizons. Spontaneity is not impulsiveness. The former is a voluntary action without external incitement; the latter is the tendency to act suddenly without reflection, because of external influence. The CEO that thinks and acts independently allows their originality, imagination, self-reliance and resourcefulness to develop.

Spontaneity is a measure of how much we are internally driven. The degree that we are externally influenced is in direct proportion to our conformism. To worry about superficiality and trivia is to cocoon ourselves in the culture of what others consider is best for us. The CEO with the courage of their convictions is unafraid to say what they believe, make mistakes, or be radically innovative in the interests of the company.

Developing volitional responsibility means reinventing ourselves to become permanently self-employed team players. Metaphorically speaking we are each our own CEO with a lifetime contract. This requires us to set an example in our own lives. It means being proactive, instead of reactive. It involves investing both time and energy in our own personal research and development centre; establishing our own strategic planning division; setting up a human resource department to make sure that we receive continuous training initiatives that improve customer relationships and quality control.

Being responsible for our future requires determining a vision and thinking strategically. To embrace such responsibility of our own volition means it is not possible to apportion blame. If what we do sparks insecurity and the need to blame we must ask if what we are doing is what we really want to do. Volitional responsibility involves having command over our actions: Events do not control us; it is our estimation of the event that we allow to affect us.

Having balance in our life is related to how optimistic and enthusiastic we feel when expressing what we do: our vocation. If we are not, then it is a clear signal that our lives are out of vocational balance.

Optimism and enthusiasm go hand in hand, emanating from the same source; one feeds the other. It is not possible to be enthusiastically pessimistic. We achieve more in our lives when we are in balance, so it is important to generate enthusiasm wherever it is lacking. Enthusiasm differs from person to person, but we each recognise when another has it. They believe in what they do and their conviction is infectious.

Each of us has a responsibility to monitor our transformation. Deep down rest our inner scales that can guide us when we are out of balance: We simply must become aware by gauging how uncomfortable we feel about something. When we do enjoy vocational balance we are on the right path, in command of what we do and in tune with the world.

After Note

Before…
a business becomes noteworthy, everyone involved works concertedly in tune together: the world loves harmony.

A piano has 88 notes. Using notes from *A Brave New Business World* supports development of your business.

A chord is made up of several notes. Creating a chord to communicate with colleagues will stimulate new ways of seeing things.

When these notes resonate…
strike a chord for your company composition…
founded on…

Respect,
Responsibility,
Reputation,
Retention,
Resourcefulness,
Referral,
Reliability,
Recommendation…

The world wants to hear it.

Value First; Always

Colin Turner is author of numerous books published in 45 languages including the international No. 1 *Born to Succeed*. As a Thought-Leader his ideas have inspired millions, influenced 1000s of businesses, and directly improved 100s. As an entrepreneur he has founded enterprises in property, services, leisure, entertainment, food and retail. Colin Turner Associates are Trusted Advisors that specialise in introducing strategic Game-Changers. He has been a President of a NASDAQ company, and holds several Chairmanships. As Professor Emeritus of Entrepreneurial Leadership he is the Creator of *The Psychology of Corporate Entrepreneurship* and *The 1% Solution*. His CEO Bullet is read and recommended by over 5,000 CEOs. He can be visited at ExpertTrustedAdvisor.com